From Jesus,
with Love

Acknowledgments

I would like to thank those who made this book possible by sharing with me the messages they received from Heaven. Although these were their own personal words from the Lord, they were willing to let me publish them for the benefit of others. May God richly bless them.

Maria David

Compiled and edited by Maria David.
ISBN # 3-905332-02-7

Table of Contents

Introduction

"The words that I speak to you are *spirit*, and they are *life*" (John 6:63). That's as true today as it was when Jesus said it to His disciples of old, and it's also just as true of the fresh, new words He speaks to His children today as it is of His words that we read in the Bible.

Jesus speaks today? Yes! He is "the same yesterday, today, and forever" (Hebrews 13:8). He will speak to anyone who believes in Him, sincerely asks Him to, and then accepts by faith that what they "hear" in their heart are truly His words. This is known as "the gift of prophecy."

This book contains over 150 short, soul-stirring messages of love, comfort, inspiration and guidance, all of which were received directly from Jesus in answer to people's prayers for themselves or fellow Christians. But like Jesus' words that we read in the Bible—all of which were also first directed to someone else—these words can speak directly to *your* heart and meet your personal needs too!

The people who received these personal messages in prophecy have all graciously consented to share them with you, that you may also benefit.

Some passages are inspirational in nature, while others offer solutions to specific problems. Some may seem like they could have been written for you alone, and some may not seem to apply to you—at least not right now. Whatever the case, all of these messages have one thing in common: They express Jesus' great love and personal concern for His children.

The key to this book is *faith!* It took faith for ordinary people to ask Jesus to speak directly to them with messages of love, encouragement, and guidance; it took faith for them to receive and record those messages; and it will take faith for you to believe, apply, and benefit from them yourself.

The Bible tells us that faith comes through reading God's Word. (See Romans 10:17.) So as you read God's words in this book with an open mind and heart, and ask Him to give you faith to receive, believe and apply them, He will!

You will then find that *From Jesus—With Love* will draw you closer to His heart of love, and help you to know, love, and appreciate Him as never before!

––––––––––––––

You too can receive the gift of prophecy and hear from Heaven for yourself or others. If you would like to learn how to tap into this unending source of divine wisdom, counsel, comfort and instruction, read *Hearing from Heaven* in the *Get Activated!* series. (See the inside back cover of this book for details.)

God's Forever Love

I remember when I formed you. With great care and special attention I handpicked each talent, each gift, each characteristic, each fiber of your being, until the combination was exactly the right portion—each specification perfectly in sync to accomplish My will and My purpose in your life, and in the lives of all those you were to touch on the great journey of life.

I remember the moment when I breathed into you the very breath of life. The love welled up so intensely inside of Me, I could not contain it! For I knew the joy you would bring, not only to Me, but to those who would cross your path along the road of life.

I love you from everlasting to everlasting, and in you I am well pleased.

———————

*E*njoy being you, because you are wonderful! Enjoy being you, because you are full of life! Enjoy being you, because you have so much to pour out to others. Enjoy being you, and enjoy My life that I have given you.

Please accept and trust that these Words are with love from My heart personally to you. I love you, and I pray for you, that not only will your faith fail not, but that your faith will grow—your faith in Me and in yourself. I love you.

---

*I*magine that there is a scale before you. I took My Own Son, the One who is dearest to Me, and I laid Him on one side of the scale. It tipped so far to that side! Then I took you, with all your weaknesses and your shortcomings, your problems and your idiosyncrasies, and all the things about yourself that bother you so much and that you think make you of so little value and so hard to love and not worthy of My love, and I put you—just you—on the other side of the scale. And the scale was perfectly balanced.

I saw that it was a good trade, to put My Son on one side, and you—just you—on the other side. I saw that it was worth it to trade the life of My Son for you, that I might have you forever. It was worth it to give My Son just for you. This is how great My love is for you.

---

*M*y eye has been upon you since before you were formed in the womb. I have been with you every step of the way. I have watched you. I have loved you. I have cared for you. You have never been out of My sight.

How I long to pour My love upon you! How I long to draw you to My bosom! If you will take time with Me in prayer, and listen to My voice in your heart and through My Word, I will show you My great, great love for you— love which is greater than the ocean, which stretches further than the horizon, which the whole universe with all its stars and galaxies cannot contain, which reaches out of understanding into infinity and eternity.

———————

$\mathcal{I}$ am the good Gardener. I have planted a beautiful, wide, glorious garden of special flowers. In My garden, each flower is different and unique, special and beautiful to My eyes. Each one serves its own purpose and has its own place in the garden and in the heart of the Gardener.

You are unique to Me. You are a special flower in My eyes. I know all about your gifts, your talents, your battles, your weaknesses, and all the things that bother you about yourself. I know about the nagging problems that you can't seem to overcome. I know your spiritual strengths and your spiritual weaknesses, your idio-syncrasies and all the funny things about you that make you an individual. I know your heart's desires and your secret longings.

I know about the times that you compare yourself to

others. I know about the times that you think negatively about yourself, when your weaknesses bother, embarrass and discourage you. I know about all these things and I love you anyway.

---

*L*earn to see My hand and My love even in the smallest things of your life—in the supply of every small need, in the keeping of your health and strength, in the keeping of the safety of your children. These are tokens of My love to you. Your children's love for you is a manifestation of My love for you, and the care and concern of others is a manifestation of My love for you. My Words are a manifestation of My love for you.

I know you, I see you, and I care about you. I care about each of your heartbreaks. I care about how you feel. I care about what you think. I care about the difficulties and hardships that you face. I care about your children. I care about your health. I care about your struggle for finances. I care about your material needs. I care about the things that you need for your children and the repairs that your vehicle needs. I care about your spiritual struggles. There is not one detail of your life that does not concern Me.

*M*y love is manifested to you in every joy and pleasure that you feel in life, in every supply of your need. Every time someone gives you love and encouragement and affection, this is My love for you.

Every time you go to My Word and you find strength and inspiration to go on, this is My love for you. When you lie down at night and are so tired and weary from your many labors, and you find sweet sleep and refreshment to your body and your spirit, this is My love to you. In your times of relaxation, when you find recreation and enjoyment and laughter, this is My love for you.

In every new thing that you learn, and every new experience that you have, in every way that you find satisfaction and joy and challenge and contentment of heart and rest of spirit and comfort to your body—all this is My love to you.

The more that you recognize Me in these everyday affairs of your life, and the more you learn to appreciate these little things that I give you and these little ways that I manifest Myself to you, the more you will grow to know, appreciate and feel My love.

───────────

*F*ear not, My beloved, for I love you with a love that is endless. Nothing that you can do or say will change My love or cause Me to withdraw or withhold My love. When you fall and make mistakes and do the wrong thing and disappoint yourself and others, when you follow far off, when you mock My Word through disbelief, when you do not reverence Me or have the love that you should have, when you think negatively and get discouraged or entertain jealous or critical thoughts, these things do not cause Me to love you less.

Your failures and problems and weaknesses do not lessen My love for you. They cause Me to weep for you, but I continue loving you just the same.

You can never be too bad for Me. Nothing you do or say or think could ever be so bad that it would cause Me to love you less. I do not put conditions on My love, saying you must be this way or you must be that way in order to receive My love. I give My love to you unconditionally. I promise you that no matter what, come what may, you will have My love in great abundance.

———————

*M*y love is like a river that flows abundantly: It never runs dry, and you may receive to your capacity, according to your need.

Fear not that it will be used up, for My love is never used up. Fear not that you will lose it, for My love is never lost. Fear not that you will be unworthy, for My love is not earned, it is received. Behold how I love you just the way you are. Yes, I know your faults. Yes, I know your weaknesses. I see when you stumble and fall, but that does not alter My love for you.

Does the love of the parent for his child lessen when the child falls? It is but increased, for he takes that child into his arms and loves it more than ever, and cares for it more tenderly. Even so is My love for you, for you are the apple of My eye.

———————

*H*ow much you see or feel My love in your life depends on your faith. I pour forth constantly, without end. The flow of My love in your life is always rich and free and abundant. I do not withhold under any circumstances. How much you see and feel this love in your life is dependent upon your faith, how much you look for the manifestation of My love, how much you are willing to believe, how much you are willing to see it, how much you are willing to recognize it in the innumerable ways that I manifest My love each day. But whether or not you see it or feel it or recognize it, does not change the fact that My love is constant and abundant and unconditional.

You cannot deserve it or work for it or be worthy of it in yourself, for I give you My love as a free gift. I love you because I love you—it's as simple as that. I love you, and I will never stop loving you, and I will never love you any less. I will always love you with a perfect love, with an unending love, with an abundant love.

I long for you to partake of this love of Mine in all its richness, beauty, power and glory. My love for you is forever love.

*N*othing will break the bond of love that I have with you. Nothing can come between us. Nothing can separate Me from you, for My love is stronger than anything. No floods can quench it, no doubts can remove it, no lies can tarnish it, for it stands stronger than any of these.

As you seek for and discover My love, as you swim in My love and in the ecstasy and the joy that I would give you, you will understand why the martyrs were even able to die for this love. It was greater to them than any trial, any persecution, or any problem. It was so strong that even at the moment when they could not feel it, they knew it was still there. It was stronger than any circumstance or any trial. These pass away, but My love will not pass away.

If you will seek Me with all your heart, you will find Me, and I will draw you to Me. As you seek Me in the Word, you will find Me.

———————

*I*f you do not feel or see My love in your life, it is not My fault nor My doing. It is not because I have withdrawn My love. How My love is manifested in your life depends upon you. Do you have faith? Do you believe? Do you truly desire My love? Are you willing to do whatever it takes to have My love? For I have said, "Draw nigh to Me and I will draw nigh to you."

I am here waiting, eager to pour My love upon you in great abundance. But I must first see your desire, your faith, your drawing nigh to Me, your belief and your willingness to recognize the manifestation of My love in your life.

---

*Y*ou are Mine and you cannot be lost to My love. You can never be despised by Me. You never slip out of My presence for a moment. You are never abandoned for a split second. There's never a moment that I am not continually aware of you. There is never a fraction of a second that I am not caring for you. There is never a thought in My heart that is unloving toward you. You are Mine forever, My child whom I love and for whom I would give My life endless times.

---

*M*y love has no limit. For I *am* Love and I cannot be contained. My love breaks forth on the right hand and on the left! You come to Me with your cup waiting to be filled, but I wish to open continuous channels of My love to you. If you will look to Me, seek Me first, put Me first, and draw near Me with your whole heart, then you will overflow with My love. Your cup will not be empty, but will overflow continually. You will not only have your own, measly store of love, but the bountiful, immeasurable store of My love to share with others.—Then, as you give, more shall be given to you, for there is no limit to Me or My love.

———————

Once upon a time there was a man who owned great riches, and as he was walking, he saw a glorious pearl of great price. The man said in his heart at that moment, "I must have that pearl!" And to buy it, he sold all that he had, all of his possessions, that he might obtain that precious possession.

Thus you are to Me. You are that pearl of great price that I saw, and I determined I would leave everything, I would leave My throne in Heaven and come to Earth, that I might have you, that you might be Mine. For this reason I sacrificed everything that I had, that I might obtain you.

———————

My love will never fail you. I've been through so much with you up until this point, I'm not going to give up now. Nothing can ever quench My love for you, for with each passing day, it only grows stronger.

I have loved you from the beginning, and I love you now, and I always will. My love never dies, but lives on and on. My love for you never grows old, but only stays fresh and new. It's never boring, but is alive and vibrant, pulsating and passionate! It never sleeps but only lives to awaken your heart. It's now, it's always, it's forever. My love is something you can lean on. It will give you strength to carry on. It will sustain you when you feel weary, and lift you when you feel you cannot go on.

My love longs for you, it weeps for you. I long to help you. I long to comfort you. My love believes in you. My love counts on you. Please don't ever doubt My love for you. I love you now, and I will love you forever.

---

*M*y dear one, I love you from the deepest part of My heart. My thankfulness for your perseverance, despite many hardships, reaches from one end of the heavens to the other. Though your heart has been broken many times, I have put it back together each time.

All have weaknesses and shortcomings, but I love no one any less for these weaknesses. My love is unconditional. That means no matter what condition you are in, whether you are doing poorly or whether you are doing well, I love you no less or more for the way you are. My love does not depend on glowing statistics or a fine record. I do not love you any less because of your failures or mistakes. My love is perfect.

Therefore you do not have to fear that I love you any less because you do not seem to be as strong as others, or because you are not the way you would like to be, or you are not as victorious as you would like to be.

When I look at My children, at the creations that My

hands have made, I just look at *them,* not their past, present or future. I just look at *you.* I love you because I made you. I do not see anything else. So come to Me and to My love. You will always find more than enough love, abundant love, in My arms.

---

*W*hen I gaze upon you, I see not the blemishes. I see not the faults and the failings, for I love you. As one who is in love overlooks the things that others may find fault with, because of his love, so it is with Me.

I am even as a blind man who sees no faults or failings, who sees with the hands, and touches and feels the softness, and smells the cleanness and the perfume, and hears the words of love, and knows just from this that his wife is beautiful and lovely, having never even seen her. Though she may even see herself as homely, he sees not this way. For he feels the love and he touches with his hands, and he feels the softness and the beauty. So it is with Me when I gaze upon you. For as one who overlooks the faults and loves in spite of them, so am I. As one who overlooks the blemishes and loves anyway, so am I.

---

*U*nconditional love is love that sees the diamond in the rough. It is love that is willing to mine jewels—

extract them from the ground, smooth away the rough edges, buff them up, and polish them with tender loving care until the brilliant stone shines bright and beautiful for all to see. Mining jewels takes time. It takes patience. It takes faith and a large measure of unconditional love to bring forth the shining brilliant jewel that lies deep within the Earth.

My unconditional love loves the unlovely. It loves the difficult to love. It loves the sad and the lonely. It loves those who are struggling, those who are lost and in confusion. My unconditional love gives and gives and gives again, and expects nothing in return.

My unconditional love is without partiality. It doesn't say, "But this one does not return My love, does not react, therefore I give up." My unconditional love keeps on believing and never gives up hope; it's enduring, unfailing.

My unconditional love knows no limits and it has no stopping place. My love will go to any length, suffer any agony, walk through any storm to love and bring one lost, lonely, battered soul through to victory.

God's Forgiveness

*M*y precious one, My repentant and forgiven child, I have seen your tears. I have felt your remorse. Come into My arms of forgiveness and mercy and let Me wipe away the sorrows of condemnation.

He that is forgiven for much also loves much, learns much from past mistakes, and learns to forgive others for their mistakes. The eyes of criticalness are converted into eyes of love and forgiveness, knowing how much you have been forgiven for. You have been given a new lease on life, a new outlook, a new vision.

---

*E*veryone has done things they feel sorry for, and maybe you've done something that you feel very bad about. You regret it and are having a hard time overcoming that spirit of sorrow or remorse over past mistakes. You wish that you could go back and change things, do it all over again and not make those same mistakes. You review those scenes or mistakes from the past, and the spirit of remorse or regret overwhelms, discourages, and condemns you.

But I do not condemn you. I do not look at the past or past mistakes and remember them against you. I do not look at you with condemnation in My eyes. If forgiveness has been sought and forgiveness has been given, then remorse, regret and sorrow must be put in the past. Otherwise Satan continues to use these things to stop the flow of My love.

You must not allow the Devil's spirit of sorrow, guilt, or condemnation to overcome and overwhelm your life. You must simply seek forgiveness and allow yourself to be forgiven. Once you've done that, there's no reason to be sorrowful. It doesn't mean that you haven't done something for which you're sorry, but that you do not continue in a spirit of sorrow.

I no longer remember your sins against you. I blot them out of My remembrance because I love you. I have heard your prayers and I have forgiven all your sins. Accept My forgiveness and be free from condemnation. Accept the cleansing power of My blood that washes away all your sins.

---

*I*n times of darkness, I will be your light. In times of sadness, I will be your joy. In times of struggle, I will be your deliverance. In times of weakness, I will be your strength. In times of question, I will be your answer. In times of doubt, I will be faith unto you.—And more important than any of this, I am love to you. I love you and I forgive you.

So do not be discouraged or disheartened. Do not look back. Do not be remorseful over the mistakes and sins of the past, for the past is the past. I have covered those mistakes and sins, and that which was scarlet shall be made white as snow. As far as the east is from the west, so far have I removed your sins from you.

In the very moment that you seek My forgiveness, in the very instant that you call out to Me, I immediately grant My forgiveness, and there is no more need to worry or fear or carry the burden yourself.

---

*O*h, My dear one, won't you come to Me now and look into My face? What do you see? Look closely and carefully. Do you see in My eyes condemnation and anger? No. In My eyes I have nothing but love and tenderness and forgiveness for you.

In My hands that I reach out to you, do you see that I want to put upon you weights of guilt, condemnation, remorse and blame? Is this what I have in My hands for you? No! Look carefully. My hands are nail-pierced. What I have for you in My hands is forgiveness, for I have already paid the price. I have already taken upon Myself all your sins—those of the past and those of the future. I have taken your sins upon Myself. Even at this moment I remove from you the weight of blame and the remorse of guilt and condemnation.

I now take this weight off your chest, and I put in its place a white dove of forgiveness. I put in its place My warm, soothing balm of love and understanding. I have put in its place the blood that I shed for you on Calvary when I gave My Own life so that you might find forgiveness, so you might find freedom and peace of mind, so you might be delivered from the burden of having to pay for your own sins.

Won't you please receive this white dove of forgiveness, and the soothing balm of My love, and the healing and cleansing power of My blood which was shed for you? Oh, won't you see that at this very moment there is peace for you?

Behold, I am the Good Shepherd. I gave My life to save the lost. I laid down My body to heal the broken. I suffered all this, not in vain, but so that I could draw you, My children, to My bosom, and comfort you and love you and give you forgiveness, redemption and healing.

I have My arms outstretched, and in My hands are precious gifts to give to you, My children, you, My broken ones, you who are suffering, you who are crying, you who are aching. I have precious gifts for you—gifts of love, of forgiveness, of mercy, and of healing. All of these things are in My hands and I will freely give them to you if you will only reach out and receive them by faith.

These gifts are not earned by your goodness. You could never be good enough to receive these precious gifts in My hands. But I give them to you freely if you can only reach out by faith and receive My love, My mercy, My forgiveness, and My healing.

———————

*I*f you were to stand before Me now, you would be so engulfed and overwhelmed by My love, that all the hurts and the pain and the misunderstandings of the past and the present would completely vanish. So great is My love for you that there is no room for sorrow or condemnation. If you were standing before Me, you would feel only total acceptance and total love, because you would know that all is forgiven. There is no fear with Me. I wash away all fear, and there is no fear in My love.

Even though you are still in human flesh, trust that My love for you is no less than when you shall arrive Here and stand before Me. I am no less distant now, and you are every bit as much in My presence. You are just as much forgiven and there is nothing held against you. You are My dear one, My beloved.

———————

I am so in love with you that I overlook all your faults and failures. I am blind with love—love that sees beyond your shortcomings and mistakes, love that only sees the good and the possibilities that others do not recognize.

I do not have a great big stick standing by ready to wallop you at your slightest failing. I do not stand ready and waiting for you to trip and fall that I may whack you back in line. How could I? For I, too, walked in your shoes. I, too, took on the cloak of human flesh that I might know and feel and understand everything about you. I know the frustrations you feel, your every longing, the incapability of your human flesh, and even your secret sins. I feel your humanness, and because of this, I have promised that I will have mercy upon you. My thoughts toward you are thoughts of peace, forgiveness, long-suffering and compassion.

---

*D*on't talk to Me about your mistakes. I say to you, what mistakes? What faults? What failings? Don't throw the past at Me—for to Me there is no past. I can't say that you have faults or weaknesses, for at this moment I see them not. When I look at you, when I look at your heart, your weaknesses to Me are no more. They vanish because of My great love for you which overshadows everything. So don't even try to talk about how bad you are, because it's not going to work. I love you too much for that.

---

*H*ow I love you. How I long to have you Here in My arms forevermore. My love for you is patient and kind. I do not wish to drive you away.—I cannot bear the thought! I am not a taskmaster that would whip you into Heaven. I am gentle and slow to anger with those who love Me. My paths are those of mercy and truth to you who keep My testimonies. In the multitude of My mercy I do gather you. I would never ever seek to drive you away. I shower mercy and truth on those who devise to do good.

My way is the way of mercy, and thus I have said, by mercy and truth iniquity is purged. This I give you, My beloved, that by My mercy and by My truth, you may find the way.

Loving Your Neighbor

$\mathcal{I}$wish to teach you greater love, to open your eyes to unconditional love, that you may learn about it, that you may partake of it, that you may apply it, and that you may learn to love others unconditionally.

I wish for you now to look upon each person as I look upon them—with endless love, immeasurable love, love that is past understanding, forgiving love, understanding love, unconditional love—that you may learn to love as you have been loved.

Learn to love others with the same kind of love that has brought you through many tight places—the love that has given you strength to go on, the love that has helped you to forgive, the love that has helped you to open your heart—My love.

$\mathcal{R}$eceive My gift of love for others. How do you receive it?—Just as you would receive any gift from Me. You ask, you accept, and you believe. How do you enact it?—One step at a time in one deed of love followed by another, followed by another.

Receive My anointing and enact it day by day, step by step, deed by deed, word by word, action by action, love by love. As you put forth an effort to give and to share and to love, I will match you abundantly, and I will pour into you a greater love, a new love, and a strengthening love.

Therefore be not afraid, just receive. Open your heart and say, "Yes!" Open your heart and say, "I want it!" Open your heart and receive, and it shall bring forth fruit in your life, in the lives of those about you, and in the lives of those you see and touch.

———————

*T*here are many ways that you can show My love to others. You can give a warm greeting instead of an indifferent glance. Take a moment to answer a question with consideration and sincerity, instead of in pressured haste and a busy rush, making others feel belittled or in the way.

Forgiveness, mercy, tenderness, gentleness, acts and deeds of kindness and caring, simplicity, thoughtfulness, rewards, words of love, words of encouragement, words of praise, all the positive and good things that you can say about someone, loving touches, giving of yourselves, taking time to talk, taking time to listen, making time to share, helping to carry the load, small acts of consideration, stooping to help the other—these will show My love.

*W*hen others fail you or make seeming mistakes, instead of blowing up in anger and frustration, say, "I pray for these and I love these. I want to help them and make it easy for them." Think thoughts of love toward those who frustrate you. Pray for them.

As you think these thoughts of love and pray these prayers of love, so will the love in your heart be able to permeate your spirit and overcome the pride and selfishness.

———————

*T*here are two ways: the way of resistance, or the way of yieldedness. The way of yieldedness is the easy way. For as the two goats meet on the narrow mountain path, and the one lies down and lets the other walk over him, this is the way I would like for you to be. Otherwise there is only confrontation and the butting of heads. It is so much easier just to lie down and let the other pass over you. Let it pass, I say, let it pass.

Things could be much easier if you would yield—not only yield to Me, but to others, esteeming others better than yourself. You must learn this basic humility, simplicity and love; then I can use the gifts that I have bestowed upon you.

Strive to be humble. Strive to be loving. Fight for kindness and understanding, for these are great jewels that you can wear, which will bring forth the true beauty

of God. Seek to be simple, to be loving, to be gentle. It is
there, I know, for I know your heart well. I know that in
the wellsprings of your heart these desires to be loving,
to be humble and sweet and kind, long-suffering and
understanding are there. But they can only be released
from your heart as you shed your pride and selfishness.

———

*T*here are many hindrances to love, but I will show
you how to break down the hindrances. I will show you
how to remove the obstacles, and I will help you to be a
vessel of My love.

First you must let Me fill you up. A vessel that is
moving cannot be filled; you must be still. You must
provide the time for Me to fill you. You must be an empty
vessel with open mouth, still and waiting for Me to fill
you up.

Do you think you can pour love out of yourself? You
will find very soon that your own love will be found
wanting. As you rub one against another, the idiosyncrasies and the quirks of another will frustrate you and you
will say, "Where is this great love that I am supposed to
have?" You cannot do it by yourself, for even the little
things will irk you. But you can do it in My power. As you
fill up on Me and My glorious love, you will have more
than enough, and this love will pour out on everyone
you meet.

As you spend time with Me, you will go forth from

your chamber with My love shining on your face! Those who see you will know that it is not of you, but it is of Me. For this does not come from your own might or your own power or your own habits or your own knowing how to love. As you retire into your chamber and spend time with Me, I will teach you to love.

――――――

I am the Creator of all things, and I judge the heart of man. I know the heart of man and all that is therein, so My judgment is just and true. At the Day of Judgment when you stand before Me and your life is reviewed, I shall judge by the act and by the intent of the heart, thus I judge righteous judgment. For I know the heart of man and there is nothing hid from Me.

When you seek to do a thing, know that I see and understand the thoughts and intents of your heart. So in all that you do, be motivated by love—My love, love for one another and love for Me.

Keys to Happiness

The happiness of the spirit is far above the happiness of the flesh, for the happiness of the spirit is something you will always have with you. It is something that will never end. The loneliest nights or the darkest clouds can't take it away from you.

The happiness of the flesh is temporal and a fleeting feeling.—It comes and goes with your mood, with your surroundings, with the physical things that you see, touch and feel. But the happiness of the spirit comes from knowing that I am your Savior, and that I care.

The happiness that I give is as constant as the sun. When the sun sets at night and disappears beneath the horizon, do you worry that it has left forever? Do you say to another, "There is no more sun in our lives"? No, it is constant, always there. Though the night comes and you cannot see it, you never doubt its existence, nor that it will rise the next morning. So is the happiness of spirit—though ever-present, the night comes and you lose sight of it. That is the time to trust and rest until morning, until it comes into sight again.

*T*he joy of the Lord is your strength. How do you get this joy? It's actually very simple: Love Me with all your heart, with all your mind, with all your strength, and also remember to love others. Don't worry about what others may think or their opinions. Just do the loving thing and the humble thing. In fact, people will love and respect you more for that.

Remember to show outgoing love and concern for others, and I will fill you with My joy, My peace, and My happiness.

---

*W*hen men's hearts are empty, they are unhappy and unfulfilled; they desire to be happy and to satisfy the hunger that they have. They look around and they see that which is appealing in the world, and they try to fill their vacuum. But what they do not see or understand, is that in order to receive the full benefit of My promises, they must fulfill their part.

This is not easy for some, for they think they will find no happiness in laying down their lives in sacrifice or in surrendering their all to Me. They do not see how that could make them any happier or fill the vacuum that they have in their heart.

But those who give their all in love for Me and yieldedness to My Spirit—laying down their lives in unselfishness—experience the true joys and ecstasies of

My Spirit, which are beyond comparison with anything in this world. This satisfies the heart like nothing else can. It fills the need and satisfies the hunger. But the only way this comes is through full surrender and yieldedness unto Me.

―――――――――

*T*he feelings and emotions you experience are a direct result of the choices you make, the thoughts you choose to think, the times you choose to be unselfish, the times you put yourself in another person's place and allow your heart to be broken and moved with compassion and love.

Feelings of love, unity and happiness are My rewards. They are given to you according to your choices and your decisions—how you have determined by your own free will to act and give and respond and sacrifice and understand.

―――――――――

*T*he joy of the Lord is your strength! It is My will that you find great joy and great pleasure in serving Me and loving Me. It makes Me happy when I see you enjoying yourself, when I see you happy and laughing. I love to see you laugh. I love to see you happy. So be happy and enjoy yourself and enjoy life. Enjoy your meals, enjoy your house, enjoy your recreation, enjoy your work, enjoy your times together. For in enjoying these, you are enjoying Me. I love to see you happy. So be happy. Don't be afraid to laugh and enjoy yourself.

---

*T*hough I open My arms and call all to come—to yield themselves to Me and let Me fill them with My love, My happiness, My anointing, My fulfillment, and My strength—very few choose to come and give their all to Me.

But, oh, if you only knew! If you could only see what I long to give to you. How I long to hold and to comfort, to fulfill your every desire, to make your heart burst with joy, overflowing with My love to pour out on others. In this is true happiness and true fulfillment.

---

*M*y child, you feel you do not have much to give. But when you look at those who have nothing and know nothing, you will understand how rich you are—how truly wealthy you are in the spirit.

Consider this: Imagine how you would feel if you did not even know Me. What if you did not even know that you would come to My arms when you die? What if you did not even know that My unconditional love is there for you, even when you feel it not? What if you did not know that rewards await you for all that you have done for Me? What if you did not even know that there was any purpose to life, that there was a Higher Being, a Power greater than yourself that could provide you with answers, healing, miracles, guidance, strength, and love?

Imagine if you did not have any of these things. Then after putting yourself in that position, take a look at your life again and realize how you are truly rich and increased in goods—the goods of My Spirit—My Words.

———————

*S*ubmit yourself, your spirit, your heart and your life to Me, and I will give you happiness. I will give you the things that will make your life fulfilled and joyous, and you will rejoice with great rejoicing.

Walking with God

The key and the secret to success—whether in this life or in the life to come—is that the more you are one with Me, and let My love and Spirit guide your every move, the more you are able to accomplish and the happier you are.

Let Me show you the secret of instant and perfect connection with Me. At any moment, any time, if you feel yourself slipping just a little, your courage fading, your spirit falling, your happiness and joy being lessened through some encounter, through some words you have heard, or through the attacks of Satan, stop for a moment, halt everything and concentrate on Me.

Focus your mind's eye on a mental picture of Me and then slip out of the work mode. Slip out of the business gear, away from accomplishing, away from the busyness, away from working. Slip down out of the mind, into the chambers of the heart. Open the door to the chamber of

My love and walk softly in, for I wait for you there. I do not ask for a long stretch of your time, but only short moments consistently throughout the day.

This is the secret, slipping away to be with Me throughout the day, keeping Me ever-present in your mind and thoughts in all that you do. As you slip in and out of My presence, you take with you a little more of My glow, of My aura, of My wisdom and power and Spirit. And this aids you in your work and in the decisions you make.

———————

I love your desire for Me. The more that you desire Me, the more I desire you. For I have said, draw nigh to God and He will draw nigh to you. I love all My children; every one is dear and precious to Me. But I spend more time with those who want Me and who love Me.

When you are stopping and calling upon Me, it creates a vacuum in the spirit which I will fill. For as I hear your voice calling Me, My attention is drawn to you. I come to you and love you and speak to you and fulfill your needs. For as I said, ask and it shall be given to you, seek and you shall find, knock and it shall be opened to you. So when you ask for Me to come, when you seek for Me, when you knock at My door and say, "Oh please, I need You," then I am there.

Seek Me and you will find Me. Ask for Me and I will be there. They that love Me most shall have the most of Me.

I am there for all, but they that call upon Me with their whole heart shall have Me. They that seek Me early shall find Me, and they that call My Name shall have Me.

———————————

*T*his is the paradox of God, that those who are weak in their own strength shall go from strength to strength, and those who think themselves strong shall go from weakness to weakness.

You must look to Me for the strength that only I can give you. You must be willing to put away your strength for My strength, for your human strength is but weakness in My eyes, and it must also be so in your eyes. Each person must realize this for himself.

Before you lies strength and weakness. I will give you My strength if you will trade in your strength that I have called weakness. Choose this day. I shall give bountifully to you if you shall be willing to give your life that others might live. For he that seeks to save his life shall lose it. This is the paradox of God.

———————————

*Y*ou are as a jewel that not only reflects light, but warmth—warmth of spirit, warmth of understanding, warmth of comfort, warmth of love. But understand and remember that the true warmth of God, the true comfort of God, the understanding of God and the love of God, comes from abiding in Me, in My Words, and letting them and Me abide in you. For it is not possible to pour forth the love, understanding and comfort of God without being full of Me.

So learn to rest in My arms, to fellowship with Me, to receive of Me, to drink in My Words and My Spirit and My love.

You must draw near to Me so that you may become full to overflowing, and so that My Spirit may pour through you in great abundance. How can you do this? By loving Me, by seeking Me, by drinking in My Words, and by believing, by yielding, by enacting and doing those things that I say you should do. For it is in these little tokens of love, these little acts of obedience, that you will learn to draw close to Me and to do those things which I tell you to do, and so you shall become filled with Me and My love and My Spirit.

Let Me cup My hands about you, so My warmth can be absorbed by you, so that you can reflect My light, and so My warmth will emanate upon others through you.

———————

*T*hroughout all the ages of man, the struggle has been between leaning upon the arm of the flesh and the strength of man, and leaning upon the power of God. All of My children from the beginning until now have had a struggle between leaning upon their own strength, and leaning upon Me. They have not fully understood that I wish for their service to be done through My power and My strength and My might.

They have not fully understood all that My power can do through the power of prayer, through the power of My Word, through the power of My direction. The power and might of God is so strong, yet My children do not tap into it nearly as much as they could.

Have I not said, "When you call out to Me with a whole heart, I will answer"? "Ask and you shall receive"? "Seek and you shall find"? "Knock and it shall be opened unto you"? These are not mere words of man, these are the promises of God! Avail yourselves of My promises, and believe, and you shall have strength and might and power that you know not of!

Talking to God

*T*hink about this: How would you feel if you never received any communications from the person you loved? Wouldn't you feel left out? How would you feel if you never received a love letter from the one who was dearest to you, not even a quick note? Or how would you feel if you went about your entire day and your spouse hardly said one word to you?

When I don't receive any word from you, it breaks My heart. It makes Me wonder if you really care and if you need Me. Communicate and do not forget Me, for with such sacrifices I am well pleased. Prayer is communication.

――――――――

*P*rayer is not the least you can do, but the very most that you can do. Think about it. If it's the most you can do, then why don't you pray more?

Prayer is powerful, and if you want My power, then you must pray. What is prayer? It's your link with the Divine. It's communication. It's tapping into the Source.

It's faithfulness to the greatest duty of man. Prayer is rest, faith, complete trust.

Prayer brings down My peace upon you. Prayer gets action. It lifts you up. Prayer changes the course of history. Prayer heals. Prayer revives. Prayer restores. Prayer builds. Prayer is humility. Prayer is My love. Prayer moves My hand and spurs Me to action. Prayer gets results. Prayer is saving grace for mankind.

Most importantly, prayer makes us one. Prayer melts us together, so that you might partake of My powers.

———————

*T*here are many ways to pray. There are times to pour out your heart to Me in desperate crying, seeking Me in fervent prayer. There are times to sit quietly, serenely, in humble seeking and sweet bidding, whispering your needs and requests in My ear.

There are times to pray as you go, petitioning from your heart in silent words, and there are times to stop, putting all else aside to seek Me with strong prayers. All are important and all have their place and purpose.

It's not the position of your body that matters, but the position of your heart. Pray long when it's needed; pray quick when you must run. There is a time to pray quick and a time to pray long, and you must learn to avail yourself of both. Pray fast or pray slow according to the need—but pray! Depend on prayer. Live your prayers. Be not weary in prayer.

$\mathcal{T}$here is nothing hid from Me. I know your every thought, your every desire, and every secret prayer. Every time you look up to Me and cry out to Me, I am near. I hear your prayers, and My heart is moved with compassion. I never harden My heart. I never get tired of listening to you. I never turn away. I never sleep. I never have a "Do Not Disturb" sign on the door. I am never distant. I am never too tired or too busy for you. I always hear and answer your prayer—sometimes in the way that you would desire, and sometimes in ways that you know not, or in ways that you cannot yet see. But I do hear and I do answer!

$\mathcal{C}$ome! Come up to the mountains, where the streams are clear and fresh. Come up where the air is not polluted. Climb ever upward, leaving the things of this Earth behind you, and you shall find a purity of spirit, a purity of heart.

Come to Me with your cup in hand, and see if I will not pour out to you some of the fresh water of My Spirit. For if you will look to Me in prayer, if you will seek Me, and if you will ask Me to pour out My Spirit to you, then I will pour forth.

Will you march upward? Will you shed the things of Earth that hold you down? Will you set your affections on things above? Will you look to My face, and My face

alone? Will you drink of My well and of My well alone?
Will you come to Me that I may pour out to you the
beauties of My Spirit?

———————

*P*ray, pray, and pray again. I love it. I want it. I need it. I
revel in it. I love to stay in close communication, so we
can be one. All your prayers are important. Some have
different purposes, but all are important, so pray.

I want to be in constant communication, constant
touch. Avail yourselves of every means, every way
possible, and let Me shower you with My spiritual wealth.
All that is Mine is yours for the asking, from a well that
never runs dry. Why settle for the human when you can
have the Divine? Receive My power! It's here. It's ready.
It's waiting for you.

———————

*S*hort prayers, long prayers, group prayers, private
prayers, desperate prayers, quick prayers, silent prayers,
walking prayers, lying-down prayers, morning prayers,
noontime prayers, evening prayers, in-between prayers,
prayers for your needs, prayers for your wants, prayers
for protection, prayers for your healing, prayers for your
work, prayers for your travel, prayers to gain victories,
prayers of deliverance, prayers to be comforted, prayers
for guidance, prayers for My wisdom, prayers for more

love, prayers for miracles, prayers for difficult situations, prayers for others, prayers for yourselves, prayers to change history, prayers that change hearts—shoot them all right up to Me.

———————

*T*ouch Me in the morning. Touch Me in the evening. Talk to Me throughout the day. Love Me and praise Me. Don't get too far away. Don't let the gaps between your time spent with Me become longer and longer. Keep in touch all the time, with just a word, a look, a prayer.

Set aside a time each day just for us. A time that you can look forward to. A time when you can just rest your body and lie in My arms. A time when we can talk, when we can laugh, when we can cry. Whatever you wish to do, whatever you wish to say to Me, tell Me. I will be there for you. I wait for you.

Listening to God

*I*n the quiet chambers, as you take time with Me, as you draw away from everyone, I'll whisper to you and speak to you. At first it won't even be audible. I'll just give you the peace that you need. I'll whisper Words of love in your ear to comfort your heart.

But as you take this time with Me more and more faithfully—always coming in faith, believing that I'm there, waiting for you, that I enter with you into the secret, quiet chambers of your heart—as you do this more and more, you will begin to hear Me more clearly. It's something that you need to make a habit of, something that you have to practice. It's a muscle that you have to exercise—that of tuning your spiritual ears so that you can hear My voice. It's just like learning something new. At first you have to concentrate, really make an effort, and you can hear it or see it a little bit.

It's like a musician learning to tune a guitar. At first it's very difficult. Musicians have to really tune in and concentrate to be able to tell which notes are offkey, which strings need to be tightened and which need to be loosened. But after a while, it becomes second nature to them, and they can do it almost without thinking.

So it is with learning to listen to Me and hear from Me. Come regularly, step into the quiet chambers of your heart, and tune in to hear My voice. Whisper words of love to Me, and wait for Me to whisper Words of love to you. Little by little you will begin to hear Me clearer and clearer, until pretty soon it won't be such a big effort. You'll be able to step quietly into the room and you'll hear Me loud and clear. You won't even wonder if it's Me. You won't even have to strain to hear it, but My still small voice will just be there, clearly instructing you in your heart.

I broadcast all the time. You just have to learn how to tune in and receive it. I have given the gift of hearing from Me to anyone who wants it. It's free. It's like a radio station, broadcasting all the time, and anyone who has a receiver can tune in and pick up the sounds, the music, the broadcast. I have placed a receiver within each person. All you have to do is learn how to use it. This requires effort, so don't be discouraged if it's not real clear right away. Keep practicing, keep coming back to Me. Keep waiting in faith, and you will begin to hear Me more and more clearly.

*A*s the world becomes more complicated, you must have Me to get you through the maze of these complications. You must look to Me for guidance, direction and help. I can show you things that you cannot see with your eyes. I can show you many things that you do not know. The world will marvel at your wisdom, at your knowledge, at your understanding, if you will but seek Me and hear from Me.

So do not be afraid to ask. Were you afraid to ask your father or mother questions when you were young, when you didn't know the answer and you needed to know? No. You had no fear, you just asked and they answered. So it is with Me.

Become more sensitive to Me and to My Spirit. Keep your spiritual antenna upward, always listening, for I have much to say.

———————

I will teach you to hear My voice. For the time is coming when this will be of great importance—a time when you must tap into My power and My resources. But those resources are there now at your disposal and bidding. So ask and seek and believe.

When you are so full of your own ideas and your own plans and are so determined, and not willing to stop, to look, to listen, to go slow, to be prayerful, you miss being in the right place at the right time, and doing or saying the right thing to the right person. Then My plan is foiled and there is disappointment. But, oh, what great joy and rejoicing there is when you step into the plan of God, and it all works well. There is great rejoicing and great happiness both in the world of the spirit and within you, when you see the answer to your prayers, when you see the power of God.

I love to hear you call on Me. I love to hear you seek Me. I love to see you take what seems to be precious time to hear from Me. And when you take the time to hear from Me, I will take My time to answer, to give you solutions to your problems, to supply your needs, to give you above and beyond what you could ask or even think. I have never failed, not once. Not since the beginning of time to this day have I failed to hear the requests of the lips of My children, and answer them.

---

*G*ood morning to a fresh start! Everything is clean. Everything is new—except My love for you, which has been from the Beginning. It is more today than it was yesterday, and it will be more tomorrow than it is today.

Here I am by your bed as you wake up, ready and waiting to love you and listen to you. What would you like Me to do for you today? I am here, waiting to help you. What questions do you have that you need help with? I just love to help you and answer your questions. What problems would you like Me to work out today? Is there any place you'd like Me to go? Any errands you'd like Me to take care of? Any heart you'd like Me to change? Here I am, just waiting to help you.

I was your servant while on Earth, and I am still your servant. Whenever you need Me to do something, just speak up, because I'm always ready to help. I'm still giving answers, still giving solutions, still working things out, still working miracles. Do you have a complicated situation? All things are simple to Me. Before you tell Me your problems, I am ready to give you the solutions. Long before you wake up I am waiting beside your bed with the solutions already prepared, if you'll come and talk with Me a little bit and let Me give them to you. I love you.

I wish all My children would be so insatiable that they would desire to hear My voice and to be fed at My hand; that they would ask Me for the direction that they need, the guidance that they seek; that instead of stumbling in the darkness they would ask Me for the light to light their way. For I am a great light, but I can only shine upon those who seek and those who ask.

How much better it is to find the way in the light than in the darkness. How much better it is to put your hand into Mine and to let Me lead you where you should go, than it is to try to find your own way and to stumble down the wrong roads and through the wrong alleys and have to backtrack, or to get lost in the brambles and in the bushes. How much better to ask Me, your Guide.

Why do you not ask? Are you ashamed? Are you afraid? Do not fear, for have I not said, "Ask and it shall be given to you, seek and you shall find, knock and it shall be opened to you"? These are My Words. Have I not said, "Call on Me and I will answer you and show you great and mighty things that you do not know"? These are My promises. Have I not said that they that love Me most follow closest? If you love Me, you will spend time with Me. If you spend time with Me, you will speak to Me. If you speak to Me you will listen, and I will speak to you and show you the way. Thus you can follow Me closely.

———————

*A*bide in Me and I in you. As the branch cannot bear fruit of itself, neither can you. The more you call upon Me, and the more you look to Me, and the more you lean on Me, the more fruit you can bear for My Kingdom.

If you will walk with Me to the garden of prayer, I will speak to you and I will reveal things to you, to lead you into greater fruitfulness and greater truth. But you must make that effort of sitting at My feet, being patient to listen and to hear the Words of truth and life that I have

to share with you, that you might be more fruitful, and
that you might look even more to Me in the days to
come.

---

*I*ntimate are My Words that I whisper in your ear. For
as I breathed upon My apostles and disciples of old and
said, "Receive the Holy Spirit," so I will breathe into your
ear My Spirit, My Words, My instructions, that you might
have the power to fulfill what I have commanded. For the
Words that I speak to you are spirit and they are life. By
listening to them you will have faith to climb mountains
and overcome obstacles. You will have faith which none
other can give.

My Words are life and spirit to you. Therefore listen to
My instructions, as one who is in love listens to the
whispers of her lover in her ear. I will whisper in your ear
My Words of comfort, My Words of love, My Words of
personal instruction for you.

---

*P*ray and ask Me to give you a sincere hunger to hear
My voice. Let My voice guide you and sustain you and
keep you close to Me.

My Words are powerful. They are life, they are truth,
they are energy. They will give you the strength and the
grace to carry on. They will give you the answers and the

solutions to every situation. They will supply your every need. They will provide direction and guidance and counsel. They will support you when you feel weary or weak, and they will sustain you when you feel faint. They will provide peace when you feel confused and tired. They will provide energy and grace when you feel you cannot go on.

Draw on My Words. Pray desperately, and I will come to you. I will answer your call. I will come quickly to you and fulfill your need.

———————

I pour out many streams of My Word in a rich and abundant flow. I have given you free access to the treasure vaults of Heaven—all yours for the asking. I unlock the storage vaults of Heaven. I give free access to My living Word, for you have need. For Earth is where the spiritual battle is being fought, and on Earth is where you have need for My direct guidance, My explicit orders, My wealth of wisdom and strategy to win the spiritual warfare.

To you, My beloved one, I give—only to be released by the hand of your faith—access to the storehouses of Heaven, that you might find help and strength, leading and guidance in your time of need.

*D*on't be discouraged if your first efforts are difficult, if you feel that you don't hear Me. Just step quietly into the chambers of your heart, into the place that I love best—the secret place of your heart that was made for Me. Step in quietly, and wait there until My peace fills your heart. Wait there until you feel My perfect peace, My comfort, satisfying your longing. Then come more often to listen to My whispers, and little by little you will begin to receive more and more from Me.

Reading God's Word

*B*ig or small, no matter what the problem, the answer is to let My light in. The secret to overcoming is My Word. Whatever the shortcoming—be it excesses, impatience, laziness, unfaithfulness, forgetfulness, worldliness, pride, comparing with others, jealousy, doubts—whatever the fault, whatever the weakness, whatever the blunder, the secret to overcoming is My Word. The secret to lasting victory is My Word. For when one is truly touched by My living Word, it gives lasting power and strength to those who partake thereof.

Do yourself a favor and feed on My Word. Then give My Word to others who are in need of help. Share My Word, give My Word, walk in My Word, talk about My Word. Live it, breathe it, exude it! And if your brother or sister falls, help them up through My Word.

———————

*F*ew people take sufficient time to rest in My arms and find strength from My Spirit and My Word. This is what I want you to do for Me—spend time in My Word. You will find faith, peace and rest as you absorb My Word. As a newborn baby cannot grow or be nourished without resting in the arms of his mother and drinking the life-giving milk from her breast, so you must rest in My arms and drink of My Words, and grow in faith by absorbing My Word.

This is a necessary part of your growth in My Spirit, to walk with Me, talk with Me, listen to Me, be rooted and grounded in Me and My Word, establishing yourself in the faith. Be very careful that the cares and burdens of this present life and world do not crowd out your special time with Me.

$\mathcal{F}$ill up your heart, your soul and your mind with good things—with the instruction, counsel, inspiration and answers from My Word—which will cause the evil seeds of discouragement, fear and despair to wither, vanish, and melt away.

Lift your eyes to Me. Open the windows of your heart and soul and let My light, love and power flood into your heart, and once again renew you. Take hold of My Word with a believing heart, with a willing mind, and receive it.

Cling to My Words, for they are as a strong pillar to which you may hold as the waters and torrents of the deep splash and whirl about you. My Word is as a high rock upon which you may stand firmly, resting assured that the foundation is solid.

*M*y gift to you is the master key to unlock the treasures which I have long desired to give you. The time is now. The key is faith and the treasure is My Word.

I do not wish for these riches to be for you alone. It is My desire that all My children partake of My treasures. But to give to others you must first receive it yourself, accept it, and believe it. Take it in and let it become a part of you. Let it fill you until it overflows on others, until it pours out your eyes, your ears, and your mouth, to all who pass by.

———————

*Y*ou must saturate yourself with My Word, that it may fight for you and wash away the seeds of doubt that Satan has planted. You must soak in My Word, absorb it and live in it, for you have been exposed to much pollution of the Devil. He seeks to hold you down, but you can be free from all confusion, darkness, and doubt. For I have promised that the entrance of My Word gives light, and it gives understanding.

So prove Me now. Take My Word into your bosom. Drink it in. Absorb it. Live on it. Let it cleanse you and wash you and free you from the pain of the Enemy. Turn not into his hands and go not his way, but keep your face toward Me.

Set My Words before you—post them on your walls, set them by your bed, carry them in your pocket—for My

Words are truth and life. Absorb them, listen to them, talk of them, think of them.

---

*Y*ou cannot shut your eyes and ears and take in nothing from this world, for this world is all around you, and you are *in* this world. But if you do not want to be *of* this world, then you must cleanse yourselves with the antidote of My Word, so that you become clean through the Word which I have spoken to you.

Heed My Words—listen to them and believe them— for Satan has desired to have you, to defeat you—not by a great flood, but by a little here, a little there; a little weakening; a little chipping away of the foundation here and there; a little disbelief here, a little doubt there; a little of your own wrong conclusions.

My Words are life-giving waters. They cleanse your spirit. They nourish your soul. They strengthen your mind and heart, and they draw you close to Me.

---

*B*e a bearer of My Word in your heart, in your mind, and on your lips. Let My Word fill you to overflowing, so that you exude its warmth, its cheerfulness, its love, and its positiveness. Live according to My Word and the love that is in it, for My love is synonymous with My Word. As you let it fill your heart and mind and spirit, it will come out of you. It will be what others feel when they are around you. It will provide an aura of love around you that others will want to be around and partake of.

I have given you the written Word, begging you, crying as a father cries over his lost children, saying, "Believe My Word! Follow My Word! Trust My Word!" If you do so, such great things are in store for you—such wonders, such joys, such ecstasies! But so few follow with all their hearts. Many follow with trepidation, with fear, and with uncertainty. Follow they do, but not with a whole heart. Oh that you would follow with a full heart, and then you would have joy and fullness of life!

I am able to restore you and to give you peace of mind. Rest on My Word and it will keep you. Think on My Words and they will cleanse you from all fears and doubts and afflictions of the Devil. Study My Word, old and new. I am able to give you the peace, comfort, strength, and freedom from fear, worry and doubt that you need. Only I am the source of peace, for I am peace, and I am love.

You must simply come to Me and rest completely upon My Spirit and upon My Words. I simply ask that you come, that you call upon Me, and let Me work within you.

Let My Words work within you, and let My Words give you strength and faith. For nothing else can give faith. It is My Word, and My Word only, that can give you faith. My Word is the source, and can supply all of your needs.

----

*A*re you believing, and thus receiving? Or are you waiting to receive so that you can believe? It is your faith that pleases Me. It is your faith, the fact that you believe and stand upon My Word, that draws down the blessings that I have for you. The blessings come no other way, for you must believe in order to receive.

I ask you to stand upon My Word, believing in the unseen, and thus you will receive and your faith will be increased. You will see that he that stands upon My Words and all that I have spoken, is he who receives My blessing, who sees miracles, who sees the working of My Spirit and who rejoices to see My hand move upon his life.

So if you wish to receive, then believe and count it done. Read My Word, believe it, stand upon it, and you will receive My blessing. You will then know that My Word is true. There's only one way to find out, and that is to put it to the test. Stand upon it, trust in it and see Me move. See Me work, and see Me pour forth My blessings upon you and your loved ones, and upon your life.

$\mathcal{C}$ast all your cares upon Me, for I care for you. This is My promise to you. But the reverse is also true. For if you do not have the faith and trust to commit all things to Me, and cast your cares into My loving hands, then I am not able to care for you as fully and completely as I would like to.

When those who are strong in the Word and rich in faith step out on My promises, trusting Me completely to provide and supply their every need, I am able to meet them, fulfill My Word, and work wondrous miracles. But those who have not had sufficient Word, who are weakened and lacking faith and trust, are not able to step out in full faith, for they lack the faith to believe that I am able to meet them. And because of this lack of faith, I am not able to meet them.

How I long for My children to be strengthened in faith through their feasting on My Word. Oh, what a simple answer—almost too simple, it would seem to some. Yet what a mighty door this little key is able to unlock. For it is the passageway into the world of My blessings, and to My answers to their prayers.

$\mathcal{T}$o you, My children I grant a touch of Heaven, that it may live in your hearts. Day after day, in many ways all around you, I touch you with Heaven—touches of love in a world that is cold, touches of supply in a world that is found wanting, touches of understanding, compassion and mercy, in a world that is indifferent.

I give you many of touches of love, in many ways, shapes and forms. But the greatest of these touches that I do shower upon you are My life-giving Words, for these Words are spirit and they are life; they are love and they are Me.

Praising God

Oh, that My children would be children of praise! Oh, that they would constantly have a word and a song of praise in their hearts and on their lips! For when you are praising, then I can envelop you in My Spirit. Praise helps to ward off the attacks of doubts, fears and worries put in your mind by the Evil One. Praise brings great strength, because praise helps you to keep your mind on Me.

You say, "Show me how to please You." I say: Sing to Me. Sing to Me with thankfulness. Sing to Me with praise. Sing to Me with love. Sing to Me with joy. Sing to Me with desperation. Sing your prayers to Me. For in My realm there is much singing. There is much heavenly music that worships Me, that sings praise to Me, that sings prayers to Me!

For those who say, "Oh, I don't sing well," I say that I hear in the spirit. I hear the songs of the heart, and not only the melody of the mouth. So do not be afraid to sing to Me and to praise Me in song. For I love to hear your tender words, your praising words, your thankful words, your words of desperation, your words of dedication to Me, your words of love. I love to hear them as you sing them to Me, and pray them to Me, and think them to Me.

---

*T*he words of praise that come from your lips, from your heart and from your spirit, to My heart and My Spirit, are the joy of My life. Send them at all times. Speak them any time to Me. Never be ashamed or embarrassed or afraid to express how thankful you are for Me and for My love.

I love each and every one of your words. No matter what you say, I understand. Even though you feel your words are inadequate, I understand. All the words that you say to Me mean a lot to Me. Every expression of praise and thanks thrills Me and satisfies Me.

---

*P*raise is so important. Praise is precious. Praise is valuable. Praise is the way of God's Kingdom. Praise is the opposite of the way of the world. The Devil brings his people into bondage through fear, worry, contention, bitterness and murmuring. But I long to bring My children into freedom through praise and giving thanks.

I find great pleasure in the praise of My children. Just as you find great pleasure in the compliments and praise of your loved one, so do I find great joy in the praise of My Bride, the Bride of Christ. As you praise Me for My blessings, for My supply, for My protection, for My Words of love, for My guidance and instruction, I will open the windows of Heaven and pour out all these things in greater abundance.

———————

*D*o you wish to be more loving? Then love Me. Do you wish to be more thankful? Then thank Me for My blessings. Do you wish to have more of an attitude of praise? Spend time praising Me. Do you wish to overcome the vices that grip you? Spend time with Me, loving Me, praising Me and worshipping Me, and I will grant the desires of your heart.

You do not need to worry, fear or fret, for as you love Me, I will abolish all worries. As you praise Me, I will chase away every fear. As you spend time with Me the darkness shall flee. For I dwell in the praises of My people.

———————

*M*y Spirit brings great joy and happiness and freedom of spirit, so do not quench it. Allow it to burn.

In your joy, praise Me. In your joy, worship Me. In your joy, sing to Me. Your children will see your joy and your happiness in Me, and they will want it and they will seek for this. They will also find their happiness in Me as they see you come alive in My Spirit with My joy, with My freedom, with My praise, with My songs on your lips. They will see the transformation of your spirits and they too will rejoice and partake of the freedoms that I give.

Therefore, rejoice! Be glad. Sing a new song to Me—a song of gladness, a song of happiness, a song of freedom. I wish to free you with My love, free you through My Words, free you with My strength, and free you with My joy.

Serving God

I love every one of My children. I love each one so much that I gave My life when I died on the cross to save each one. My love is so great that many do not understand it. Many cannot see how I could have come to Earth and died on the cross to save you. In this day and age, people question whether or not I really am the Son of God, and whether I really am who I say I am. So, it is in the hands of people like you that I leave the responsibility of giving this message to the world.

I need your help to spread the news that I am the truth, I am love, and I am the only light of this world. This day and age is getting darker and darker, and the world is being flooded with so many lies that it is difficult for people to understand the simplicity of the Gospel and the simplicity of My love. It is for this reason that I have chosen you to help give My Words to the lost.

———————

*M*any shall be surprised when they come into My Heavenly Kingdom to see the great importance of love, the hidden, unseen acts of love and the giving of love. For to love is more important than the many things that you think are so important.

This is a day of choice. This is a day of challenge. This is a day when I am saying to all of My children: How much will you love? How much will you think of others? How much will you give of yourselves? How much will you give up your own personal plans, your preferences, your immediate desires, to be able to give love to those who are in need?

I have no eyes but your eyes, no lips but yours, no hands but yours. Much of the love that I show can only be shown through another. Much of the comfort and encouragement and affection that I wish to bestow can only be given through another. My love can best be shown through you.

———————

*I*t is time to look outward, not inward. You must not become secluded in your blessings, looking inward only to yourself. You must look outward to those who suffer, to those who thirst, to those who are hungry and to those who are desperate and in need and dying. They are dying spiritually without My Words, without My truth. You have an abundance, so give of your abundance.

Give, and it shall be given to you. I will pour My love upon you and I will give you great strength and anointing as you go forth to preach My Gospel, My Word, My love. Thus you will heal their hearts.

---

*A*t night when you go to sleep, think about the love that I have bestowed upon you. Count your many blessings and you will see how in so many little ways and through so many little things and through so many people I have extended a kiss, a touch, a word, a blessing. There are so many ways that I have loved you personally.

But I ask you also to think about how much you have given love. What have you done to show love to another, that they may also be touched by My love? Haven't I said that there is greater joy in giving than in receiving? There is so much more love in giving love than in receiving love.

How much do you give to those who I also love? Remember that I have no hands but yours, no eyes but yours, no heart to touch others' hearts but your heart.

Give and it shall be given to you. As much as you have done it to the least of these, you have done it to Me. Therefore be touched by My love and touch others with My love.

---

*L*ift up your eyes and look on the fields of the world, the fields of mankind, for they are white and ready to harvest for My Kingdom. The harvest is plenteous and the trees are laden with ripe fruit. Even now the fruit falls to the ground and perishes for want of those to harvest it. Lift up your eyes and look upon the fields. Do not be secluded in your blessings, but let your heart be touched with the feelings of those who do not know the truth of My love and who do not know Me, their Savior, those who are dying of starvation and who freeze in the cold for lack of the warmth of My Spirit and My love.

Therefore do not say there is yet more time, but give My Word. Sow the seeds of My Word and reap the harvest.

———————

$\mathcal{L}$et Me use your eyes to see the needs of others, whether great or small. Let Me use your ears to hear the heartcries of the lost. Let Me use your tongue to pour forth My Words of love and of compassion, of prayer and of encouragement to one who is cast down. Let Me use your mind that I may implant My thoughts therein— thoughts of love and of kindness. Let Me take your heart in My hands and let it break for the multitudes of people who have not yet heard of My love. Yes, let Me break your heart, that I may afterwards pick up all the pieces and put it back together again as a softer, more useful vessel that My love can pour through.

Let Me use your hands to dry the tears of those who are crying, to give a pat on the back to those who are discouraged, to be a helping hand to someone who is falling by the way. All you must be is willing, heeding My gentle whispers, and I will put these situations in your path. They may seem small and insignificant, but they are great in My sight. It is a high calling to be a vessel of My love.

———————

*F*reely you have received, freely give, for I have given much unto you. I have poured into you, and now I send you as a vessel full of the waters of My love, full of the elixir of My love, full of My healing balm to pour on others. Be a vessel that pours out. Do not be one that withholds and contains, but be an open vessel that freely gives, even as you have received.

As you pour out, I will replenish, and your vessel shall not run dry. I will fill you up to overflowing as you overflow upon others. For unto whom much has been given, of the same shall much be required. This I require of you: that you love the Lord your God with all your heart, with all your mind, with all your soul, and that you love your neighbors as yourselves.

As you pour out, pour not out in your own strength, but simply open your vessel so that the elixir of My love may flow out of its own accord, that it may be drawn out by the vacuum of others, by their need for love.

———————

*A*re you willing to reach out to these who are buffeted in the storms of confusion—these who are caught in the snares and brambles, who find no joy, no power, no happiness in day-to-day life? These who are caught in the thick of battle, whom Satan tries to confuse, that he may snuff out their light?

Will you be a vessel of My love—My never-ending, never-failing, never-swerving, unconditional love for these? How I love them. How I long to wipe away their tears and their heartaches. How I long to melt away their confusion. Who will heed My call? Are you willing? May I use your hands, your arms, your mouth? Will you yield your members to Me that I may love these who are weary, who have lost their enthusiasm and joy? I have no hands but your hands to lend a tender touch. I have no arms but your arms to extend a comforting hug. I have no mouth but your mouth to speak a word fitly spoken, that it may encourage and lift them up.

I have no smile but your smile that sheds a little bit of sunshine through the dark, stormy clouds on a rainy day. I have no feet but your feet to walk a mile in their shoes. I have no body but your body, to reach out, to love, to comfort, to hold on to and to pray for these, My little lambs.

How far will My love go?—To the ends of the Earth, to the highest Heaven, to the deepest depths of the sea. My love will walk out of its way to love and win one lost child who is groping in a sea of confusion. My love is the rescue boat; My love is the lifesaver.

———————

*T*here are many occasions, even in your everyday life, where I wish that you would stop and touch and listen to and pray for others. Have I not given you the sample of the good shepherd who leaves the ninety-and-nine— the duty, the responsibility, the work, all that he thinks he must do—as his heart is pulled toward the one who cries and is in need?

For there will be many upon the road of your day; many occasions for you to recognize a need for love. Therefore stop your working and be touched by My Spirit. For as you have done it unto the least of these, you have done it unto Me.

———————

*M*y love is all-encompassing. My love is a tender touch, a loving look, a bright smile, a kind deed, a silent prayer. My love takes every critical thought and transforms it into a fervent prayer. My love wars for those who struggle in spirit, fights for them at Heaven's throne of grace. My love is a friend in need and a friend in deed. My love does not criticize or point the finger.

My love is all these things for those whom it is hard to love. My love is faith to believe that as you continue to give, I will work in their hearts. My love keeps on loving, even if you cannot see immediate results.

As My love begets love, so does the tiny spark of My love, shown through you, ignite a fire in the hearts of others. Just as love begets love, enthusiasm begets enthusiasm, emotion begets emotion, and vision begets vision.

I will be your hands, your arms, your feet, your mouth, that you may love those who are in desperate need of love. My love will cover the multitude of shortcomings. My love will melt away the coldness. My love will break through the barriers.

---

*S*pread My love wherever you go, cheering the hearts of those around you, encouraging others. For even with simple things like this I am able to use you greatly to change hearts and lives—not only the lives of those who know Me not, but even the lives of those right by your side, those who you come in contact with daily.

God's Rewards

The rewards I give you depend upon you and how you live, what you do for Me. I have made an original investment in you as an individual, and the returns that you will receive on that investment depend on what you do with it—whether you take the investment and you hide it away and bury it, or whether you use it wisely, consistently and faithfully.

You are the one who is responsible for the rewards, for the returns, and for the blessings that you receive from Me.

I am a God of love and mercy, righteousness and tenderness, forgiveness and sympathy. My rewards are absolutely fair. My judgment is totally honest. My recompense is absolutely true.

I give to each person as he has given to Me of his life and his labor, his tears and his prayers and his concern. Everything that you do for Me in this life is greatly rewarded in the life that is to come—much more than you could ever imagine. You will be given an hundredfold for every bit of love and concern and labor that is given to My Kingdom.

There is no sacrifice that will go unrewarded or unseen or unnoticed by Me, for I watch your every move and I know your every thought. I see your tears and I hear your prayers. I feel your concern, and when you struggle, I am moved with compassion for you. When you are tempted and when you are weary and weak, I am moved with compassion for you. When you are victorious, I rejoice with you. When you are strengthened and you go forth to battle, to fight against the Devil, I see, I hear, I understand, and I record these acts of valor, courage and dedication. And you will be rewarded far beyond your wildest dreams! For I am a just God and I give to each one his just reward.

---

*W*hat special quarters I have prepared in My Heavenly City for those who have given their lives unto Me fully and completely. What honor, unequaled and unparalleled, awaits them upon their arrival at the gates of Heaven.

For the treasures and rewards of the Kingdom of God go to those who have given of themselves for another— for a lost one, for a lonely one, for a sad child, for a friend in need, for an outcast, for the unlovely. The honors and medals go to those who stretch themselves to the limit and beyond.

Finding Faith

Faith is the key to the life of a Christian. It is the key to blessings, provision, power, protection, inspiration and receiving every good thing that I wish to bestow upon My precious children.

Have faith—faith in My love, faith in My promises, faith to obey in spite of overwhelming obstacles and seemingly impossible situations. For this is the proof of your love—your faith in Me, your faith in My Words, and your faith in My power to fulfill them. Your love for Me is manifested in your faith—the golden key of faith.

So guard this precious treasure I have given you, this golden key of faith. It is something that must be kept through constant care and nurturing and feeding from My Words, which are spirit and life. By believing and receiving, drinking in and partaking of My Words, you keep the golden key of faith polished, and you will be well able to use it to open many mighty doors of My blessings for all that you need in every area of your life.

---

*Y*our faith is what opens the door of your heart and life so that My love may flow in. How do you find such faith to believe and receive My love? Such faith is found in obedience. When you walk in obedience to Me and My Words and My will, then you have confidence, for you know that I will honor and bless you for your obedience, your yieldedness, your desire to please Me.

Obedience and faith go hand in hand. The more you obey Me and My Words, the more faith you have that I will bless you. In your obedience you are drawing near Me. In your obedience you are creating a vacuum for My blessings and My love. Your obedience gives you confidence to come boldly before My throne. Your obedience causes you to look around with eager anticipation, to see the manifestations of My love in your life—which you know will be many, because you know you have brought Me much joy and pleasure, as an obedient child brings to his father.

---

*D*o not look at what you do not have, but keep your eyes upon Me and have faith in My promises. Have faith in My Words to you. Have faith in My voice speaking to your heart. Have faith in the love that you feel surrounding you.

When you are tempted to fear or doubt or worry, fix your eyes on Me and trust. When you are tempted to tremble, just trust in Me. When you are overwhelmed and the tears fall, keep trusting in Me through your tears. Trust Me through everything.

Trust that I know best. Trust in My wisdom. Trust in My ability to lead you and guide you and use you to the fullest. Trust in Me for the future. Trust that I will not fail you, and that I will fulfill all of My Words to you. Trust that I will not leave you comfortless. Trust that you will indeed feel My love and know My love in a greater way than before.

Trust that I will comfort you in the night when you feel that you have no one else. Trust that I am there by your side. Trust that I am able, and will help you through this time of testing. Trust that I will not fail you, no matter what your mind tells you. Keep your eyes on Me and trust Me wholly.

———————

$\mathcal{D}$o not think that you know best, for the mind of man is not greater than the mind of God. That which seems logical to your mind is not necessarily the way of God. For My ways are higher than your ways, and My thoughts than your thoughts. It is in the acceptance of My Word, in the acceptance of faith, that there is peace and rest in spirit.

So lay down the burden of your mind. Lay down the burden of your analytical mind and come to Me with faith.

*C*reate faith through hearing My Word. Resist negative thoughts. Hear My whispers. Desire above all things to do My will. Give of yourself and lay down your life for others. Trust in Me and do not lean to your own understanding. Hunger after righteousness and do those things which you know to be right. Love Me with all your heart and all your soul and all your mind, and love others as yourself. Through such obedience to My Word and way comes faith, and through faith you will discover such love as you have never known before.

My love is there for you. What you receive and how much you receive is dependent upon your faith. Reach out the hand of faith, and according to your faith it will be done to you. My capacity to give love to you is limited only by your capacity to receive. Your capacity to receive is limited by your faith. Your faith is determined by whether or not you obey My Words.

———————

*W*hen I lay in the boat sleeping, and the storm battered about, My disciples knew not what to do, but were fearful for their vessel because of the wind and the waves. So they woke Me, for they knew that the answer lay in My power. I said, "Peace, be still," and there was peace. They came to Me, admitting that they knew not what to do, and I gave them peace.

So come to Me in faith, the faith of a little child who

knows that his father will not lead him astray, but will speak the truth to him. Come to Me in faith, laying down your preconceived ideas, laying down that which you are so certain is so. Come to Me with an open heart and an open mind, and let Me give you peace—the peace that comes from faith, the peace that comes from trust, the peace that comes from knowing that you are yielded to the will of God.

---

*Y*ou must trust My Word, for in trusting My Word, you are trusting Me. When I say in My Word I am there, then know that I am there. When I say in My Word I am your comfort, then know that I am your comfort. When I say in My Word it shall pass, then know that it shall pass. When I say in My Word I shall supply, then know that I shall supply. For My Word is truth. My Word is life. My Word is love. My Word is Me.

---

*F*aith is the true coinage of Heaven. Faith is the key that unlocks the treasure house of My blessings—My spiritual blessings, My material blessings, all of My blessings. Without faith, it is impossible to please Me, for he that comes to Me must believe that I am the rewarder of those that diligently seek Me.

Have I not promised that I would open the windows

of Heaven and pour out a blessing you could not
contain, if you would but trust Me and believe My Words
and obey them?

Your faith can release the power of the universe! Your
faith can move mighty mountains of obstacles and
difficulties! Because if you put your faith in Me and My
Words, I will move the mountains, I will overcome the
obstacles, and I will provide the solutions.

The Power of Choice

Oh, My precious, forever love, I do not willingly afflict you with pain and problems and punishment. I am a God of love, a God of mercy. Great is My mercy toward you, as great as to the heavens and to the clouds.

I am a God of love, a lover of love, a lover of salvation. I do not afflict willingly with hellfire and damnation, problems and sorrow. With great mercy and great truth I do all things well toward you. In the multitude of My mercy I preserve you.

Therefore know that many things you interpret as punishment from My hand are but a fulfilling of your own will; it is a reaping of your own choices. I am bound by My Word. I am not a man that I should lie, and as I have bestowed upon you the majesty of choice, so I am bound within these choices.

Other things that you misjudge as punishment are merely a granting of your desires and prayers. And when necessary, even the instruction that I send is all in love. For I am not an infidel, and I do care for My Own—and I only care for you in love. In great love and in great mercy I gather you to Me.

———————

*H*ear now and learn a great truth: Within the majesty of choice that has been granted to man, My hands are tied according to your will. Many circumstances and incidents are brought about by your own hand. Do not be confused between what is from My hand and what is from your own hand.

In the divine majesty of choice that has been granted to every man lies great responsibility. To you to whom much has been given, much is required. In this you are learning to be responsible for your own actions. Do not be not deceived, for whatever a man sows, he will reap. Therefore you must not blame Me for actions of your own doing.

Many things that you call punishment are just a reaping of your own actions. It is by the majesty of choice that a man willfully chooses and signs his fate.

———————

*N*o matter who you are, where you are, or what you are doing, you can choose your state of mind. You have power over your mind. Just as you can choose to say yes or no to Me, you can choose to have a strong, sound mind of faith, or a weakened mind that has been dulled and darkened by being on the wrong channel.

Those who will be the strongest in spirit and in mind and in faith will be those who let My Word live in their hearts and minds—those who live and breathe and drink My Word. Those who absorb My Word and believe it and let it become life and strength to them will continue to walk with great strength of mind, spirit, faith and heart. Nothing shall be able to quench the strength of My Word in those who cling to it and keep it always foremost in their minds.

———————

*T*he purest form of simplicity is this: Trust in the Lord with all your heart, and lean not to your own under-standing. If you would have simplicity, if you would have peace with no confusion, then trust Me explicitly. Look neither to the right nor to the left; consider no other options, but just trust. In this lies perfect peace.

When you trust Me with all of your heart and with every aspect of your life, you can know that you are in My will. So if you would have perfect peace, then trust Me.

———————

*D*o not fill up your heart with your thoughts. In any choice or any decision that you face, come to Me. Look for the answer in My Word, and seek to do what My Word says. As you base your actions and your decisions according to My Word, I will transform you and you will see My love and power flowing out of you in a way that you never imagined. This is My blessing and this is My reward.

Help in Trying Times

I have heard your prayer, I have seen your tears, and they are precious in My sight. Though you may feel that this is one of the lowest times you have ever been through, yet in My eyes it is a precious time. I feel you closer to My heart than ever before. As I hold you in My hands and behold the beauty of your tears and your prayers to Me, the beauty of your surrender and humility in coming before My feet and saying, "Nothing in my hands I bring, simply to Thy cross I cling"—as I behold this, I love you. I hold you close to My heart, and I comfort you.

But you must let Me comfort you. You must have faith to reach out and receive from Me. It is nothing that can be earned or worked for. I wish to give it to you freely because of My love for you.

You must make the decision to accept My peace and comfort. And though this time seems long, it is only a moment compared to eternity. You will be rewarded greatly for your faith.

*F*ear not that your heart breaks. Fear not for the weeping, for this weeping shall endure for a night, but then there will be joy and the sun shall break forth with shining once again in your life. The heartache that you feel shall be washed clean, and I will give you a new beginning.

As you walk down the path of My perfect will, you shall go from strength to strength. You shall feel My hand of blessing upon your life. You shall find great joy, satisfaction and love. You shall find new challenge and new inspiration in your life.

The things that you once held on to, but are now willing to let go of, shall in the future be looked upon as weights that turned into wings. You shall soar on the winds of My Spirit higher than you ever dreamed possible, freer than you ever knew possible.

———

*W*hen the storms of life blow around you, and you are tossed and buffeted and carried to and fro with the winds of distress, adversity and difficulty, come into My chambers for a little while, until these calamities be past. Come into the warmth of My arms. Rest your head upon My shoulder and see how I will care for you, and how I will stroke your brow and make these mountains of problems melt away entirely.

This is the refuge that I have promised you—the solace of My love, the comfort in My arms, the peace that flows from My heart to yours, that fills you and envelops you and transports your spirit to the heavenly realm where you see things with new eyes.

In those quiet moments when we commune together, I can change your perspective. I can give you new ideas and new thoughts. I can do so many things for you, if you would just step aside into the chamber of My refuge.

———————

I understand the trying of men's hearts, the depths of despair, of discouragement, and of desperation. I understand the depth of loss, for I had to leave My Father to go to Earth, and then I had to leave those that I loved so dearly on Earth to return to My Father.

I also understand the depth of pain and affliction, for I screamed out in agony as the nails pierced My hands and My feet. I understand the feeling of being forsaken by those who loved Me, even My Own Father, and thus I cried out, "My God! My God! Why hast Thou forsaken Me?"

I understand the depth of fear—fear of facing that which is ahead for the pain and the sorrow that it shall bring. And so I said, "Father, let this cup pass from Me."

I understand the depth of the feeling of loss, for those who loved Me most abandoned Me as I was carried away into captivity. I know the depth of hurt to see one that you love betray you, even as Judas betrayed Me with a kiss.

Have I not been touched with the feeling of your infirmities? Do you think that I do not understand these things, and that I do not have great compassion upon you? My heart breaks to see you in your pain and in your struggle, and in your trying times, your times of testing and purging. My heart breaks for you when you feel so hopeless, lost, and forsaken, when you grasp with all your might and yet you feel as if there is nothing to grasp any more.

Though My Father did not let this cup pass from Me, and though I saw My loved ones flee from My side in time of trouble, and this one that I loved betray Me, and though the nails pierced My hands and feet, and though I was beaten with many stripes, and though I felt as if My Father had forsaken Me, and though I had to pass through death—yet it all brought about such great victory, such great renewal, such great salvation!

Though all looks dark and you cannot see, know that I have My arms around you. I ask you to trust Me in the depths, trust Me in the despair, trust Me in your heartache, trust Me in your loss. If you are willing to drink of this cup, if you are willing to say, "Not my will, but Thine be done," you, too, shall have a glorious victory that will far surpass anything that you have known.

$\mathcal{I}$ love you from the depths of My heart. Though you face pain and suffering, hardship and sorrow, you can face these things in great faith, trusting Me and My Word and all that I have promised, for I will not fail you.

Trust Me, even if you endure sorrow, pain, loss, hurt

and forsaking. Know that I will never forsake you if you will cry out to Me, if you will seek Me and My Word, and if you will hold on to the crown that I have placed upon your head. If you will carry its weight, I shall reward you with great peace, great love and great understanding. I will say to you, "Well done, My good and faithful servant; enter into the arms of My love!"—as My Father said to Me when He held Me in gratitude after the sacrifice that I made and the suffering that I endured.

———————

*T*here are cycles in life when things go well, then they go bad, then I bring about victories and they go well again. You must hold on to Me, seek Me, and follow Me through each phase of life's cycles.

When you're faced with obstacles, tests and hardships, don't let them discourage you. Don't be downcast or worry that they will not be solved, or that victories will not be won; for I say to you, they will, because they are part of the cycle. But you must go through this portion of the cycle to come out at the other end with victory.

That's the purpose of the cycle: that when the problems and the difficulties arise, you rise up to meet them in faith. You fight and you win, and that brings forth the next portion of the cycle: the victory, the progress, the forward movement. Then you are faced with new challenges, new fights and new tests, and you must once again fight, take up the challenge, seek Me, and cry out to Me, that you may overcome these tests and difficulties, and that you may then move out of that portion of the cycle, and again on to the victory.

Like a wheel, the top goes down to the bottom and comes up to the top again. That is motion, and that moves the vehicle forward. That's what these cycles do— they move you forward.

So you must take up the challenges, you must seek Me, and you must win the victories, so that the cycle can be ever turning, ever revolving, ever moving forward— so that you will constantly be moving forward, growing, going on, ever upward, ever forward and on to victory!

———————

*Y*ou wonder, "Why, Lord? Why do I have to go through so many hardships and difficulties? Am I not pleasing You? I love You. Why do I have to go through these things?"

Many Christians through the ages have asked this question. In each case it was My Spirit working in them, because unless they became weak, I could not become strong in them. Unless they became broken, I could not teach them compassion; I could not give them the empathy, the outgoing concern for others they needed. I could not give them the many beautiful gifts of My Spirit that this brokenness and these hardships bring.

Through these afflictions I am teaching you to fight— not with your own strength, but with My strength through prayer and looking to Me for everything in your life.

*T*he greatness that God gives comes about from the tests, the trying times and the trusting. The strength and the power that you seek does not come in the way that you would think. It does not come in the paths of glory as with man, but through the path of God—the lowly, humble path.

So in your time of suffering , look to Me. Call out to Me! Cling to My Words! Grasp them, hold on to them, for they are truth. For you to be the man or the woman of God that I would have you to be, you must have the understanding that My Word is truth and power and strength and might. It is My Word that saves you and strengthens you. It is My Word that encompasses you about with protection. It is My Word that gives you the love that you seek. It is My Word that does all of these things. You must be connected to Me, and the root of that connection is My Word.

---

*C*ome, My dear one, into My arms. How greatly I love you and care for you. I long to comfort you and soothe your hurts. I wish to lift you from your depths of despair, to cheer your heart, to give you fresh courage, a renewed vision, an enlightened mind, and a heart with wings, that you might fly into My presence, into My love, into the temple of My Spirit.

Alone with Me in the intimate chambers you will find

the strength you need. For only in gazing upon My face and receiving Me through My Words will you find the vigor and stamina you so desperately need.

---

*Y*ou may not understand some things today because it is not My time to fully reveal to you My complete plan and purpose. Believe and trust, even though you do not understand. For My ways are not your ways, and you can never know the mind of God by trying to understand and analyze with your own mind. I will reveal My thoughts and My ways by the power of My Spirit to those who are receptive, yielded and believing, who will receive My voice with faith, love and appreciation.

I promise that if you will hold on by faith—not even knowing if you have the strength to hold on—you will not fail. Just as gold is purified in the refiner's furnace, those who pass through the hot flames of testing, are those who come out as finer gold. I test you that all the dross and impurities may be melted away. So do not fear the testing, for I purify you out of love, and I cleanse you in answer to your prayers.

---

*I*n spite of how sorely you are tested and how weary you are, as you rest in My arms and sing to Me praises of thankfulness for all that I have given you, I will open the way before you. I will lift you above the burdens and melt away the anger and frustration. I will dispel the questions as you rest in My arms and sing sweet songs of love and praise to Me. I will never leave you nor forsake you. I will never fail you!

If you lift up your eyes and your voice to Me in song and praise, in total surrender in My arms, I will give you grace and strength, and make the way clear before you. For you cannot forge the way ahead alone. You cannot carry the burdens or push away the hurt and sorrow in your own strength. Only I can do these things. I can make the mountains melt away as you love Me and rest in My arms and sing to Me your songs of praise and thanks.

$\mathcal{I}$ know that your heart breaks and aches, and you feel that this is more than you are able to bear. But My dear one, I will never ask of you more than you are able to give. I will never require more of you than you are able to do. Whenever you reach the point that you feel it is too much, that the weight of the sacrifice is crushing you, at that moment, I will reach down and lift you up. I will draw you to Me, and give you strength and faith.

$\mathcal{D}$o not look at the waves or the wind or the storm or the condition of your vessel, but look to Me, the Author and Finisher of your faith. Although the waves rise and seem so much stronger than your weak vessel, know that I am the Master Pilot, and if I am guiding your little ship, I can guide you through the waves and the wind and the storm. Oh, how I wish to guide your vessel. But in order to steer you through the storms, you must let My hands be upon the wheel, and not your own.

I am the Master Pilot, and I know how to pilot the boat in the severest of storms. I know how to face the vessel into the wind, and how to ride over the tall walls of waves that seek to crush. So let My hands rest upon the wheel, that I may pilot you through the storm and into calm seas once again.

The storms always pass, but the question is, will the tiny vessel make it through the storm? If you let My hands be upon the wheel, I guarantee you will make it through the storm, and that you will once again find the calm, warm seas. So do not look at the waves or the wind or the storm, but keep your eyes focused fully upon Me.

———————

I know it looks to you like it's really been a hard time, and it has. It looks to you like things are really messed up—you messed up, others messed up, and you ended up in a messed-up situation.

But you know what? I don't see it that way. I see it differently than you see it. There is a reason why I have allowed all of this to happen. It's another step in your growth. Every day I'm teaching you and helping you to learn more.

I know you've been discouraged and you've made mistakes, but that's okay; that's how you learn. You're learning patience, you're learning perseverance, you're learning how to make decisions.

This time is meant to strengthen you. I know it's hard, and you look around you and it just doesn't seem like the greatest situation, or like it's working out very well. But you don't have to worry, because I'm right there. You can talk to Me about it any time, every day, and if you listen, I'll talk back to you. We can talk together and I'll help you solve your problems. I'll give you the faith and perseverance that you need for this time.

———————

*W*hen you feel weak, I will be strong for you. When you feel confusion, I will give you peace. When you feel fearful, I will comfort your heart. When you are doubting, I will give you faith. When you feel strain, I will bring relief. When you feel lost, I am right here with you. When you feel useless, I will give you a purpose. When you feel anguish, I will give you joy. When you lack confidence, I will be your assurance. When you feel muddled and cloudy, I will give you clarity of thought. When all seems dark and stormy, I will be your shining light.

———————

I know your heart. I understand what you're going through. I know that it's very hard and you feel like you're at the end of your rope. You feel like you don't have the strength to go through this and come out on the other side. Don't worry about how you feel, for I know your heart. Believe Me, you will come out on the other side.

I suffer with you. When your heart aches, My heart aches. I ache for you. I hurt for you. This is one of those times when I take you in My arms and I carry you. I know that it's too much to bear on your own and that you cannot go it alone, so I hold you tight and I carry you. I hold you to My breast. I'm holding you tight this very minute, kissing away the tears and the hurt.

Believe Me, the hurt will go away and will turn into glorious blessings. Out of the ashes of hurt and defeat will grow beautiful lilies of My love—not only in your life, but in the lives of many, many others who will be touched by it. Only believe.

The path of true greatness is the path that goes through Me. I cannot make you great until you have come to Me with all of your heart, all of your soul, all of your mind, and all of your strength.

These things that you have passed through are not defeats, but they are stepping stones to glory—not the glory of man, but the glory of God, the glory of humility, the glory of utter dependence upon Me, the glory of My Spirit working through the humble heart, the trusting soul, the yielded mind, the loving spirit.

So know and understand that the things that you suffer, the hardships that you are faced with, the burdens that you bear, the testing, the purging, the trying, the heartache and heartbreak, the pressure, the squeezing, the difficulties and sufferings, do not take you away from Me. They are not a sign of My displeasure. They are not meant to show that I am not there. They are the steps that you must go through to come to Me.

But know that I am always there. In the deepest and darkest experiences and in the greatest despair, I am there. Turn and face Me and trust Me, even when all else seems so dark. Trust Me, for I take you through the darkness that I may bring you out into My glorious light—the light of My love, My truth, My strength, and My power.

———————

$\mathcal{T}$here are so many things that can and do go wrong in this life—so many broken dreams, so many visions that do not come to pass, so many things that just do not work out the way you so desperately wanted them to. Yet through all the broken dreams, your visions that do not come to pass, the things that don't work out as you had hoped they would, I am there with you. I hold in

My hand greater dreams than you've ever dreamed of, more beautiful visions than you've ever seen, and greater things than you've ever hoped for. Your heart has not imagined the fantastic things I have in store for you who love Me, for you who stick it out through thick and thin.

$\mathcal{T}$his world is too much with you. If you would only keep one foot in the heavenly realm, then your life would be so much more heavenly and your joy would be full, because My Word would remain in you and My joy would be your strength in time of trouble. You would know the joys of trusting, of faith, of going forward, of going where you had not had the faith to go before.

The cares and trials of this world are too much with you. You limit My mighty hand, which has so much to give you. Bounties beyond your wildest dreams are available to you now, My children, if you would step through the gates of praise, the gates of My Word, and would follow as I would have you follow—step by step, moment by moment, not doubting, not fearful, not complaining.

Freedom from Stress

Pressure is from Satan. He is the one that causes the press on your spirit and the feeling of discouragement. He tries to make you worry and look at the load and the work. Even though the load is great and the deadlines are before you and there is much to do, you have to resist the Devil's temptation to feel under too much pressure.

Resist his spirit of pressure by continually casting your cares upon Me. Release the pressure by looking up to Me. When the load is great, I give more grace. When the deadlines grow closer, I give greater help. I will give you all this and more, if you will continue to look to Me and cast your burdens on Me. Give Me every care, every worry, every question, every thought, every concern, every load.

Take time with Me, even if it is just for a few minutes, to release the pressure. Take a few minutes here and a few minutes there and release the pressure by singing a song, reading a verse, praising Me, speaking words in prayer to Me. Those few moments when you are looking up to Me and entering the temple of My Spirit will release the pressure and take the weight from your shoulders and put it back on My shoulders where it belongs.

No matter how much you have to do, no matter how much you have to take care of, and no matter how much you are responsible for, you are My responsibility and I will not fail you. I promise that as you look to Me for the help that you need, I will take away the pressure so that you can relax in My Spirit.

As you lean on Me and look to Me, you will feel My Spirit strengthening you. You will feel My arm helping you and upholding you. So just rest upon Me and lean upon Me and let Me uphold you. The burdens will never be too great if they are Mine. The to-do list will never be too long and the pressure will never overcome you, as long as you resist it and call on Me for help.

———————

*T*here is a time and a purpose under Heaven for all things: a time to work, a time to rest. If you will rest, both physically and in spirit, I will give you the freshness that you need, to do that which you must do. For one cannot work and work and work and never end. You must stop and rest.

If you will take time away from your work and rest physically and in spirit, you will receive clarity of mind and heart and spirit. You will receive clarity in your thinking, renewal of your spirit, renewal of your body, renewal of your outlook. You will look upon your work in a new light and see that the things that you considered so heavy are no longer heavy, because you have renewed strength.

It is not enough to rest only in spirit—you must also rest your body. Your body houses your spirit, and when the body is weary and weak and under constant strain and stress, your spirit cannot do all that it should. For together they are one, and both must rest. The body must rest in sleep and through recreation. And the spirit must rest in prayer and by getting filled with My Word. With these two together you shall have all the rest that you need, that you may be strengthened and refreshed in Me.

———————

I see your every tear. I hear your every cry. I feel your every frustration, your every worry, your every burden, your every desire. I know everything about you—all your wants, all your lacks. I see your heart and all that is in it, and I deeply love you.

I long to hold you and caress you and kiss away the hurts and heartaches, if you will but allow Me to. I long to comfort, to soothe, and to pour My balm of love upon your every heartache, your every heartbreak, your every worry, your every fear, your every tear, your every frustration. I long to blow away every cloud of confusion and to soothe your ruffled nerves. I long to melt away the bitterness and turn every deep longing into marvelous fulfillment and true satisfaction.

I long to give you the sun and the moon, the stars in the sky, the ecstasies of Heaven, and a love that will never end. I long to pull you through whatever deep, dark experience, whatever dense fog you find yourself in. Whatever confusion or frustration you have bottled up inside, I long to melt it all away, because I love you.

Strength comes not from your own spirit. Strength comes not from carnality and the reasoning of the mind. True strength can only come from Me. True strength can only come from resting in My arms, for I am strength.

I can only live through you if you are letting Me, by resting in Me, by getting your strength from Me, by relaxing, by getting refreshed each morning, and asking Me what I want to do, what I have planned for you each day, and what My will for you is. I can only live through you if you let Me live through you.

You do this by spending time with Me, by saying, "This is Your day, Lord. Do with it what You will." This is where you will find your strength.

The secret of vitality, of sparkle, of that shine on your face, of that twinkle in your eye, of the love, compassion and tenderness that others need so badly, is in refilling and refreshing yourself in Me. Only then will you have something to pour out to others. This is the secret. This sweet communion with Me will empower you to be able to give, pour out and meet the need.

The secret is spending time with Me in peaceful rest each morning and night. As you recharge and refill your cup, so will you be able to overflow on others. This is the secret, and it is My promise to you. As I promise, so do I fulfill.

So come, My precious one, for in rest and refilling in our secret chambers each morning and each evening, you will find rest. This is the secret.

Encouragement When You're Sick

Do not fear this light affliction. Just as I learned obedience to the Father through the things that I suffered, you too will learn to have a closer walk with Me through the delicate condition I have bestowed upon you. I know you, I love you, and I care for you, just as My Father cared for Me.

I, too, was afflicted. I knew what it was like to mourn. I wept. I was afflicted with weaknesses of the human flesh for your sake. I know and understand, because I experienced and felt everything you are feeling. I took on human flesh that I might understand.

Fear not for your weakness, for I have heard your prayers, I have seen your tears, and I answer. I am right here by your side to hold you and to comfort you with the same comfort that My Father gave Me.

Remember that I was a man of many sorrows and of a broken heart. Through it all, I learned the blessing of greater power of spirit. I suffered many afflictions, but through them I learned to have greater dependence on My Father. I learned that His power, and His power alone, was enough to sustain Me. There was a purpose in each affliction, in each difficulty through which I had to pass.

Through it all, most importantly, I learned to look up, to keep My eyes on Heaven. It was in My very weakness and My afflictions that I learned to avail myself of My Father's great power. I had to call on Him, I had to lean hard on Him, and in leaning I found My strength. So I grew, and I learned, and I saw that in My very weakness was the greatest strength of all.

---

*A*sk for prayer and ask for My healing, for I am the Great Physician and I am the most wonderful doctor. Not only am I your doctor, but I am your loving Savior, and I long to make you whole.

---

*B*ehold, I am the Good Shepherd. I gave My life to save the lost. I laid down My body to heal the broken. I gave all this. I suffered all this, not in vain, but so that I could draw you, My children, to My bosom and comfort you and love you and give you forgiveness, redemption, and healing.

I have My arms outstretched, and in My hands are precious gifts to give to you, My children, you, My broken ones, you who are suffering, you who are crying, you who are aching. I have precious gifts for you little sheep—gifts of love, of forgiveness, of mercy, and of healing. All of these things are in My hands and I will freely give them to you if you will only reach out and receive them by faith.

These gifts are not earned by your goodness. You could never be good enough to receive these precious gifts in My hands. But I give them to you freely if you can only reach out by faith and receive My love, My mercy, My forgiveness, and My healing.

---

*F*ear not for these battles and this affliction that you have faced. Think not that it is a punishment or a chastisement from My hand. It has only been a purification. It has only been a purging through which I have desired to bring you closer to Me, and through which I have desired to demonstrate your faith. Even in your moments of affliction, pain and great suffering, still you trust Me, still you love Me, and still you look to Me in faith. This is a great thing, a great testimony.

Fear not what others may think of you. Fear not that others think of you as a failure, or as a misfit, or as a burden, or as one upon whom the hand of the Lord rests heavily. Know instead that I have chosen to honor you and privilege you with this time of testing.

---

*S*atan desires to have you that he may sift you as wheat, yet I continually pray for you that your faith fail not. Therefore look not on these light afflictions as punishment for your sins, for they accomplish a great purpose.

These light afflictions are but stepping stones, all working together for good to accomplish My will and My purpose. They lead to the path of higher ground of fuller faith and trust in Me.

I give you these multicolored stepping stones, that in your light affliction many purposes may be established: greater dependency on Me, greater faith, greater prayer, greater encouragement as you partake of My healing touch, greater power. As you pray and trust in Me for your light affliction, it will encourage and increase not only your faith, but the faith of others as they see your sample of faith, trust, and dependency on Me in your affliction.

Relief for Loneliness

When you feel like no one cares and there is no love to be found, that is the time to lie back in My arms and find peace. When you are discouraged and feel like you're a great big mess, look into My wonderful face and see Me smile upon you, for I love you just the way you are.

When you feel worried or frustrated, run to Me, for I will be your perfect companion. If you feel that no one can possibly understand the difficulties that you are passing through, that is not so, because I always understand. I long to hear them. I long to solve them. That is the time to run to Me, to tell Me the problems, the burdens, the worries and the cares, and I will give you the solutions that will melt them all away.

———————

You were together and now you are apart. I brought you through this love relationship that you may better understand the love I have for you, and the personal, intimate relationship that I wish to have with you. It was a learning experience, and a time for you to experience and understand the depths of romance, the longings of the heart, the desire for love and how to give love, so that you may use what you have learned.

Use the love that I have put in your heart, and use your broken heart to shed My love on others. Use your hands to touch them with My love. Use your tears to understand their tears. Use your longing for love to fulfill another's loneliness. Use the gift of love that I have given you. Think not of this gift of love as a weight or a heaviness or a burden, for it is meant to be a blessing to those around you. As you warm others with your love, so will you also be warmed.

———

*I*n your loneliness, call out to Me. Though you cannot see or feel Me, you will be closer to Me and more intimate than when with your closest friend. In those times our love will grow stronger and our relationship deeper than any earthly love could ever hope to be.

In this oneness with Me will grow your greatest and most lasting happiness, fulfillment and contentment. I use the ache in your heart to start this deeper relationship with Me, which is the beginning of the deeper love that we learn to have, and that is continued when you arrive Here in Heaven. That longing to talk, for friendship, to have constant companionship, to love and feel loved, will be completely fulfilled when I return for you. But for now we can be close in spirit.

$\mathscr{I}$am proud of you for your willingness to believe My promises in spite of deep hurts and heartbreaks and disappointments. But I am not a disappointment, for I am the Lord your God. I care for you. Rest in Me and trust in Me and I will pour forth blessings upon you—showers of blessings and showers of love.

But you must do your part. You must hold on to Me and My promises. You must trust Me. You must believe My Word and you must not doubt. And in due season you shall receive all that your heart desires and all that you need.

But know this, that I am always with you. I am always at your side. Come to Me, you who labor and are heavy laden, and I will give you rest. Come to Me, you who are lonely and you who are hurting, and I will give you love. Come to Me, you who are disappointed and you who are suffering, and I will give you surcease from these things.

Come to My arms and let Me hold you close to My bosom. Let Me whisper in your ear as I say to you, "You are My love, you are My love, you are My love."

---

*M*y dear child, I know your loneliness and the feeling of being unloved. But know that I love you dearly, and that I am there for you any time, all the time. I know it is difficult in the night. I know it is hard in the times when you seek companionship and find none. But My dear one, I am your constant companion. I am your best friend. You are My Bride—the Bride of Christ.

So turn to Me in your loneliness. Set your affections on Me, and I will fill your every need, for I am He who fills all things. The day will come when you shall be lonely no more. You will be with Me forever, and these days shall be as nothing. They shall not be remembered because of the great joy and the great love and the great companionship that you shall have with Me. You shall have your heart's desires and more—much more than mind or heart could ever imagine.

Comfort When a Loved One Dies

This precious one who is so close and so dear to your heart is now safe in My arms and in My care. Therefore do not fear or weep for these ones who have gone on to their reward. They have gone on to new horizons, to brighter days. They have passed through the door to the other side, but you have not lost them. They are not gone. You have not lost their love, for they are just as alive today as ever.

Although you cannot see them or touch them or feel them or kiss them and look upon their faces, they are alive. They live! This time of separation, this time of distance between you is only for a moment. It is only for a time. Therefore do not weep, but take courage.

Find hope and comfort in knowing that I do all things well; that whether I give or whether I take away, I do all things in love; that all situations, all circumstances, every detail is from My hand. I am your Father, and I have not done this to hurt you or crush you or break you into powder and destroy you, but I have done even this in love. Though you may not see it now, it is a privilege and an honor that I have taken your darling one into My arms.

So come into My arms and rest your weary head upon My breast. Feel warmth and comfort and tenderness in My bosom. Let Me dry your tears and let Me kiss away your hurts.

───────────

$\mathcal{D}$o not weep for your little one who has flown away to My heavenly Kingdom. Do not weep for this one, for he is safe in My arms. I am protecting and keeping him and loving him and helping him, and he is safe and free and healthy and happy. For he is My precious little lamb and I have brought him Home where he can be at peace. He is very much alive and he continues on learning and growing and maturing. He will wait patiently for when you will be together again as one big happy family. There will come a time when he will once again be in your arms and you will be able to kiss him and love him and tell him all the things that you want to tell him. You'll be able to tell him all the things that you wish you had told him when he was there with you on Earth.

Before you know it you'll see him again, bright and shining and happy. Before you know it you'll be doing all the things that you love to do together, playing and running and learning. Your precious one is not far from you. He is not distant, he is not dead, he is not gone. I have only taken him to My arms for a moment that I might nurture him and comfort him, and I will watch over him until you are reunited as one.

Weep no more for your child, for he now represents you Here in My Kingdom and will be your aid and support in times of need. He loves you dearly and is proud that you were his parents during his stay on the Earth. He is challenged and thrilled to be Here in My heavenly realm. He is in very good hands. Do not worry any more, but be at peace.

---

*Y*our mother was so precious to you, such a friend, companion and teacher, and brought such joy and security to your life. I understand the loss that you feel. But do not fret, for this time when you are apart is only for a moment. It will pass so quickly, and then you will once again be reunited with great joy, love and thankfulness. You will shout many shouts of praise and thanks that you didn't give up, but that you kept trusting until the end.

I have brought this one into My Kingdom and into My arms. This loss that you feel is but a momentary loss, and the rewards which I will reward you with will be much greater. So do not fear and do not waste precious

moments lamenting and blaming yourself. Do not take
upon yourself the guilt and condemnation the Devil
would seek to place upon you. For these thoughts—the
guilt, remorse, extreme sadness, condemnation, lethargy
and blaming yourself—are not from Me. They are from
Satan, who seeks to steal your strength and your joy.

So do not fear and lament and weep, but rejoice that
the one you love so dearly is now safe in My Kingdom.
He is safe and able to perform My will and to fulfill the
purpose for which he was created.

----

*L*et not your hearts be troubled, My dear ones. I am
raising up your loved one, who was but a young boy, into
a young man now. He is a vessel fit for use in My Kingdom. He is greatly loved Here, and is a joy to many
people's hearts, for you gave him much love. You poured
into him, you sacrificed your time and energy, and gave
him much care and tenderness. Your investment is now
blossoming and coming to fruition, as your son is now
overflowing with the love and care and tenderness that
you planted inside his heart.

Building Your Marriage

To build a marriage you have to build it in spirit. Spending time with Me together is how you strengthen your marriage in the spirit. You must invest in your marriage the things of the spirit, spending time together reading My Word, praying together for your personal situations, for the children and for the needs of others. You must spend time in heart-sharing.

You must have time to just be together, to talk, to pour out your hearts, to talk about the things that are bothering you or weighing heavily on your heart, your burdens, your discouragement, your frustrations. You must have a chance to pour them out, and to show understanding and compassion, to work it out and to bring these things to Me in prayer.

You must spend time with Me, because those who come to Me and love Me in this way will be strengthened. You can't expect to have a strong, united, happy marriage if you never spend any time together, doing the things of the spirit—spending time in the Word and prayer, loving Me, singing to Me, praising Me.

*S*ometimes what looks like problems in a marriage, is actually My way of strengthening the marriage by bringing those involved to a crisis. If you handle the crisis right, by praying desperately, counseling, seeking Me, communicating honestly, then your marriage will be stronger in the end. You will be more mature, deeper spiritually, and you will understand your spouse better, through the lessons you've learned together and the difficulties you've experienced together.

───────────────

A marriage is a sacred thing to Me. When you see your wife in need and in pain, you need to be moved with compassion to pray for her, to comfort her, to show her love and sympathy and be soft toward her. Don't get exasperated and fed up, or feel put off if she is weaker for a time. Don't feel like it is a big inconvenience and it's really hampering you, but look at her with sympathy and tenderheartedness. Take her in your arms and comfort her, love her, weep for her, and especially pray for her.

If you can't have love and tenderness and compassion for this dear woman who is your wife, then how can you have love and compassion for others?

*T*ake time with Me, together with your spouse and the children. Take time reading My Word together, praying together, seeking Me together. Take time in open communication, expressing your desires. Do you have a desire to become more unified as a family? Talk about it. Do you feel you need My blessings spiritually and financially? Talk about it. Come before Me together as a family, and I will pour out My healing balm upon you and your household. I will pour out My blessings and My supply.

---

*I*f your marriage is going to be strong, it must be strong in the spirit. If it's going to be strong in the spirit, then I must be the center. Your focus, your unity, your love, all must be centered around Me. Then you'll have what you need to make it over the human weaknesses and mistakes and misunderstandings. But when you go for a long period of time without having good prayer and communication, without humbling yourselves and uniting around My Word, it's very easy to become set in your ways, proud, unyielding and intolerant. You lose the compassion. You lose the tenderness. You lose the sweetness.

---

*M*y sweet and precious one: Thank you for being such a good wife to your husband. I'm proud of you, and I commend you for taking good care of your man for so many years, and remaining faithful to him. I love to see people's love endure the test of time. I love to see people who remain faithful in their commitments to each other, and who continue to love, no matter what. Sure, there are ups and downs and tests, but you are a good example because you love each other. For this, I commend you.

It's especially beautiful when a couple lets Me be part of their union. Thank you for letting Me be part of yours.

---

*Y*ou who are married, if you will love Me together, sing to Me, praise Me, worship Me, put Me first, seek My face together and seek to hear My voice; if you will lift one another up in praise to Me, and pray for one another—you will have a new marriage, a new strengthening and a new spirit of love.

The fires that have dwindled can be rekindled as you worship Me together, as you seek Me for a renewal. But to do this, you must lay aside the old weights, the old ways, and become renewed in your relationship with Me. As you together renew your relationship with Me, I will renew your relationship.

You must humble yourself and lay aside your familiarity. You must both make a commitment to change your ways and to seek Me together, and truly become one with Me together. I will bless this, and I will renew you and strengthen you. I will return to you the fresh, new love that you once had—because you will be focusing on Me and have your eyes turned to Me. For, yea, I am Love.

As you give your love to Me, I will give My love to you, and so My love will renew you and rekindle your love for one another. You shall see new things about each other, things that you did not know. As you deepen your love for Me together, so I will deepen your love together.

I have put you together, but through familiarity and day-to-day living, you have set aside that deep communion with each other and that deep communion with Me. Renew the communion with Me together, and set aside the old ways and preconceived ideas.

Set aside all that you think about one another, and instead focus on Me together. Love Me together. Praise Me together. Sing to Me together. Worship Me together. Adore Me together. Seek My face together. Cry out to Me together. And I will fill you together. I will be one with you together, and we shall be a three-fold cord together.

---

*Y*ou who are thinking about becoming one with another, set your affection on things above together, even before you are married. Come to Me together. Set your foundation on Me.

In the days of your courtship and in the days of your wooing, woo with My Spirit. Humble yourselves before one another. Come to Me in love together. For I put that love in your hearts to begin with, that you may become a union.

Yet for that love to remain, you must focus on Me, for I am the supplier of fuel that keeps the fire burning, and you must tap into My supply together, lest the fire die. If you do not begin in this manner, loving Me together, praising Me together, and focusing your love and affection and attention upon Me together, the love will grow cold and you will be building on a foundation that is not sure.

Look at your relationship as an amplification of the relationship that I wish for you to have with Me.

———————

*O*nce upon a time, there were two beautiful, smooth, clear, clean rivers that flowed parallel to one another. But I caused these rivers to intersect, to come together and meet, and to become one.

As they flowed together and grew, behold, they came to the edge of a mountain, and these rivers that once were so smooth and beautiful went tumbling over the edge. The river tumbled ever so violently down the mountain, thrashing and beating against the rocks and the boulders. But it was through this very tumbling and thrashing that the water was purified, aerated and cleansed, and it became a beautiful waterfall that many could look upon.

The river's willingness to be thrashed about and beat against the boulders was the very thing that made it magnificent and drew people's attention to it, and caused them to marvel at the beauty before their eyes.

After this time of suffering and purging and thrashing and purifying, behold what is at the bottom of this beautiful waterfall—a deep and gloriously clear pool of cool, refreshing water! These two rivers that have united and have been purged and broken have become a beautiful pool of water.

Many people come to sit beside the pool. They dip their hands into the cool water and are refreshed and strengthened, and their battles are alleviated. They find strength and encouragement and comfort in this pool that is so deep and cool and clear and precious in My sight.

It is this pool that I am forming. This is My goal, to form of these rivers and of this thrashing waterfall a beautiful pool of refreshing water that many will come to and drink from, and there find succor and comfort and encouragement. Therefore be not weary, but hold on.

For though the rivers are beautiful, and though the

waterfall is magnificent, and many people look at it and marvel, the pool will be the most beautiful. This is when you shall come to the end of yourselves, and My plan and My purpose shall then be accomplished.

Parenting Jewels

*A*s was said about the woman in the Bible, "She had done what she could" (Mark14:8), just do what you can, and then leave the rest to Me. Trust Me for your children. If you can't give them all that you would like to every day, don't worry about it. Just give what you can, and I will care for them. I will make them what I have designed them to be. Simply be faithful with the little that you can do each day, which is a lot.

If you have My love and give it to your children, this will cover everything else. But you must take time with Me in My Word, in prayer and fellowship. I wish to give you greater power, greater peace, greater faith and greater love.

Even though you have many duties, you must make time for Me. Your strength comes from Me, and without Me you will be like an oil lamp burning without oil, and your wick will turn black. Without Me, your strength will be sapped, and you won't have peace. You won't have enough love. So make time for Me each day and I will renew your relationship with your spouse and your children. They shall see a new light upon your face.

*M*y precious one, in whom I am well pleased: Do not worry about burdens that press your children, and thus press you, but come now into My arms and find your rest. For if you are to find the rest that you need, you must not only cast your burdens upon Me, but also cast the burdens of these for whom you care upon Me. My shoulders are broad enough and My arms are wide enough to carry the load.

I see your mother's heart, how you long to comfort and hold and help each one. I see the purity of your desire, as a true mother of God who wants the best for her children. The best you can do is to cast all the burdens upon Me—your own burdens, and the burdens of your precious children—for I will carry you, and I will carry them. I will give you the solutions you so desperately need as you continue to ask Me about all things. Yes, My sweet one, you are unable to do enough. But I, in you, am able to meet the need.

———————

*F*atherhood is a wonderful thing. It will make you strong. It will make you loving, caring, responsible and supportive. Many other gifts of My Spirit it will bestow upon you. I implore and compel you to care for these little ones, so you can have My full blessing, so that I can make you the man of God that I ordained you to be and that you have a desire to be.

I know your love for your children is great, and your desire is for them to know Me in a much greater way, and to be close to My heart. This is also My desire, for I love each one specially. I have each one in My special care. Each one is a tender plant in My sight that I wish to be fed, nourished and strengthened by My Words, watered by the dew of My Spirit and tenderly cared for and guided, so that it will grow in the right direction, straight and tall and strong and healthy.

But there are many things that attack My tender plants, that attempt to destroy what I have planned for them. There are sicknesses and diseases and blights that threaten them—the sicknesses and poisons and pollutants of the Evil One, things which are not of Me or My Spirit or My ways, but are the ways of the world and of death.

Carefully and prayerfully guard and feed and tend and love, and give utmost care to My tender plants, that they may grow strong and healthy and upright, and that the blights and sicknesses of Satan do not befall them.

The Devil knows that his time is short, and he seeks to flood the Earth with his lies and pollution and deception, to pollute the Waters of Life and wash away that which is good and Godly and right and loving and truthful. Let him not wash away any of the tender plants in your care. Keep them watered, and keep their thirst quenched with the pure waters of My Words. Be diligent caretakers. Do not be weary in your love and care and feeding of these tender plants, and you will be richly rewarded.

———————

I am the Giver of all life. I breathe the spirit into each one. Each new life is a gift of love to the mother and father—My gift of love to them. Many look at it in the natural and say, "This is but a biological occurrence." But I say to you, it is a gift of love from the hand of God in the life of the mother and father.

This child is My gift of love to you. Your child will love you deeply, and you will love him. Through him you will learn of My deep, unconditional love for you—that I love you when you're good, and I love you when you're bad. I love you when you do the right things, and I love you when you do the wrong things, just because I love you.

What better way could I teach you of My deep love for you than to give you your own child to love and care for, to hold, to feed, to teach, to love? When you look at him and when you feel love for him, remember that this is how I look at you and this is how I love you. And yes, My love for you is even greater.

When you hold him, think of Me holding you. When you feed him, think of Me feeding you. Even when you change him, think of Me cleaning you up and loving you in spite of sins and weaknesses and defecation in the spirit. You will learn that it means nothing—you just wipe it away. Though it is unpleasant, it does not take away from the great love that you have for your child. As he grows and you correct him, this too will teach you.

So, My precious child, who has a precious child, know that My hand is upon you and that I have given you this gift of love. I have put him in your hands to love and care for and to teach and train. He will also love and care for and teach and train you, through all that you learn in raising him, your precious young one.

---

*M*y dear mother of My children, mother of precious little hearts, My little cherubs: Thank you for being a mother to these little loves. Great is your reward. Blessed is the fruit of your womb, and great shall be your blessings. Yours is a sacrifice of love. Has it not been said that there is no greater love than a mother's love? So there will be no greater reward than that which I give to a mother, for she gives and sacrifices of her body, and of her blood, and of her heart.

The things that man counts on Earth as the greatest sacrifices, I count as the greatest blessings, and I give the greatest rewards for. He that cares for My little ones learns the most about giving, sacrificing and loving. These are the things I place the greatest value on.

Your children do not take you away from Me; they draw you closer to My heart as I see you toil. As your labors increase, so do I give you My grace more abundantly. My heart and My hands reach out to help you more.

When your children are sick, do you not cry out to Me in greater desperation? Is your heart not more broken? Is your spirit not more humble? Do you not become weaker in yourself but stronger in Me? Do you not trust more?

All of these are not burdens, but are secret treasures you have more abundantly than others as you care for My little ones.

———————

*B*eing a father is hard work. Caring for your children is an arduous task, but it is the most rewarding task in this world. Come to Me for the love that you need. Look to My Word on fatherhood. The power of My Spirit shall come upon you, and you shall be an example to many of love, of willingness to sacrifice, and of responsibility for your loved ones. I will make you a pillar in My house if you will be the man that I have called you to be—a responsible, caring father.

Oh, if you only knew the blessings that await you, the strength of spirit that you would be given, the rewards in Heaven that you will receive, you would not hesitate to care for these little ones. Your children will bring you such happiness and give you such courage and dedication.

For what greater love hath any man than this, than a man lay down his life for his young children? They are your friends, My son, and they will be your friends all the

ays of your life. They need you. They need your father-
ng. They need your care. They need your love. They need
our understanding.

Will you take this responsibility? If you will, you shall
ave My full blessing and great fulfillment in this life. For
here is no greater fulfillment than to care for and
urture the children that you father and bring into this
vorld.

---

*B*abies—what a wonderful thing! My precious one, I
ave given you a love gift. This is a token of My love to
/ou. This is not a punishment or a judgment, but a gift!—
A gift of love! As you nurture it, you will find it will bring
/ou great joy and satisfaction.

I know it is not as you had expected, but believe Me,
:his is a gift and a blessing. Do you remember the story
about the woman to whom I gave a gift and she counted
it a burden? I had wrapped the gift in old brown rags
and told her to carry it with her as a token of My love. It
was a test to see if she would believe what I had said.
Although she carried it around all her life, she never
really looked at it or accepted it as a gift and a blessing
from Me, but more as a burden and a duty for her to
carry. So it never brought her the joy that it could have.

On that blessed day when she came to Me, we
unwrapped that gift together. To her amazement, inside
the old brown rags were jewels and unspeakable

blessings! She looked at Me with sad remorse and said, "Oh, if I had only known what was inside, I wouldn't have looked at it as a burden all those years!" My sweet child, do not be like her, but believe Me when I say that this baby I'm giving you is a gift and a blessing.

————————

$\mathcal{T}$hank you for your years of faithfully caring for your children. Thank you for pouring your love into them so freely and abundantly. Thank you for laying down your life for their sake. This is very precious in My sight.

Know that there are many blessings, many rewards and many spiritual riches of inestimable value awaiting you in My heavenly Kingdom.

Your love and sacrifice, your prayers and tears over the years have built you a mansion Here so lovely, so delicate, so intricate, so ornate, so splendid, so marvelous to behold, so enthralling to the eye, so breathtaking to the soul. All who pass by and look upon your future home see clearly the love, toil, sacrifice, unselfishness, and giving of yourself and your faithful service for Me these many years. It is a testimony of your love.

My dear one, I wait for the day when I shall have the pleasure of saying, "Well done, My good and faithful servant. Enter into the joy of thy Lord!" Your children are very precious in My sight, and very close to My heart.

Also available from Aurora ...

My King and I

Looking for ways to express your thankfulness to God? The sample praises in this book will provide you with the words to say and a springboard from which to formulate your own! Learn the art of praise today!

Discovering Truth

This two volume topical study guide to the Bible will help you quickly find what the Bible has to say on a wide range of topics related to your faith and daily life!

Dare to Be Different

A collection of inspirational and refreshingly iconoclastic essays on some of the fundamental issues of Christian life and faith. Guaranteed to challenge you to be different and make a difference!

Wings of Prayer and The Wild Wind

These two CDs will lift you into the heavenlies! *Wings of Prayer* is a collection of soothing and heart-warming songs of prayer to God, the lyrics taken almost entirely straight from the Bible! Its companion CD, *The Wild Wind*, is a rhythmically upbeat tribute of praise and thankfulness to God; its lyrics also taken from the Bible. (Available as a set or individually.)

The *Get Activated!* series

If you would like to learn more about how you can develop your personal relationship with God and receive His blessings, love, and happiness in your life, don't miss *Get Activated!*—a series of booklets covering the fundamentals of faith and how to apply them to your life today. Titles include:

Prayer Power

Hearing from Heaven

Overcoming Obstacles

The Faces of Love

Understanding God's Word

God's Gifts